GET OVER YOURSELF!

GET OVER YOURSELF!

How to Drop the Drama and
Claim the Life You Deserve

Tonya Pinkins

HYPERION
New York

Library of Congress Cataloging-in-Publication Data

ISBN: 0-4013-0176-2

Hyperion books are available for special promotions and premiums. For details contact Michael Rentas, Assistant Director, Inventory Operations, Hyperion, 77 West 66th Street, 11th floor, New York, New York 10023, or call 212-456-0133.

FIRST EDITION

10 9 8 7 6 5 4 3 2 1

DEDICATED TO
Manuel, Maija, Myles, and Maxx

My Master Teachers

| CONTENTS |

You hold in your hands a trustworthy map for navigating a life lived in integrity with your soul. Trustworthy because its author, Tonya Pinkins, has practiced every method she recommends. In my own work, I have long taught that thought—being a unit of mental energy—transmutes itself into tangible form as circumstances, symptoms, health, creative endeavor, prosperity, and relationship, impacting virtually all aspects of life as we know it. Since Tonya has been a member of my spiritual community for a number of years, I have had the privilege of witnessing how she has evolved in her practice of working with the power of thought, which today qualifies her to assist those who wish to enrich their own life experience.

Tonya compassionately assists her readers in cultivating an honest relationship with themselves on spiritual, mental, emotional, and physical levels of existence. Individual responsibility is inescapable for those who sincerely want to "drop the drama and embrace the dharma," as she poignantly puts it. The exercises she has created are practical and their results provable, dissolving barriers to the happiness that is the birthright of all humankind.

There is an evolution of consciousness taking place on the planet that we have never before experienced. Even popular news magazines headline about breakthrough discoveries connecting thought and matter, consciousness beyond mind, prayer and healing, and spiritual inclinations built right into our DNA. In Tonya's book, we are provided with an opportunity to experiment in the laboratory of our own consciousness and prove that we are not merely bystanders in life, that indeed we have the capacity to consciously cocreate our lives in alignment with the spiritual and scientific findings of our lifetime and to realize the interconnection of all life, the great something out of which we and our universe have been birthed.

Michael Bernard Beckwith
Founder and Spiritual Director
Agape International Spiritual Center
Los Angeles, California, 2005

| ACKNOWLEDGMENTS |

I would like to honor and thank a few of the people without whom this book would not have been possible. To Michelle Etlin, a living Buddha, thank you for walking with me and holding my hand through the years, for your generosity, humor, friendship, and selflessness. You make the world a better place. To Sister Morningstar for your unconditional love, spiritual direction, and intense discipline, which always allows me to do what is mine to do. To Michael Bernard Beckwith, Rickie Byars Beckwith, whose incredible music makes it all come alive; and my West Coast Agape Family, for your love and prayers and providing me with a community of truth seekers. To my editor, Leslie Wells, for cheerful encouragement, guidance, and focus. You never miss a thing. To Will Schwalbe for the title. To my friend Deborah Gregory for the subtitle. To the entire marketing and sales staff of Hyperion for making this book a tremendous success. Most importantly, to everyone who has crossed my path and by doing so made me all that I am today. Special thanks to all those who were stones in my path for providing the tools to build my character and strength.

Life is often much more simple than we describe it. Love is often much more sacred than we experience it. People are often much more helpful than we give them gratitude for. We are much less alone than we ever imagine and far more unique than our wildest dreams.

May this book, penned by a living saint, reach first your hands, second your heart, and third your world. And may the great goodness you seek reach its fullest potential as simply and sacredly as the river takes on the beauty of the forest she traverses and carries its mystery in the reflection of her waters.

Simple and Sacred ~ †
Sister MorningStar, Hermitess

Down the Path

ONE

DISCERN WHAT YOU
NEED TO LEARN

If I can set you on the path to creating what you want right now, would you be interested in that?

Yes, or Yes?

If I can set you on the path to receiving more of everything you've ever wanted, would you be interested in that?

Yes, or Yes?

Good.

When you internally answered yes to those two questions, your transformation began. You consciously set your intention to do/be/have more. Did you know that 80 percent of success is simply showing up? And here you are. So congratulate yourself for taking the first step in creating the life that you desire and deserve.

I appreciate the time you have taken out of your busy schedule. Technology, far from making our lives easier, has simply shown us how much more we can do with the time we have. Yet most of us are still playing catch-up. So I am honored that you paused—between the e-mails and the pagers and the cell phones and the children and the education and the career and the relationships—to read this manual. I said manual, not book. Manuals provide instructions on how to make things work, and that's exactly what, by purchasing this manual, you showed up to do: to make your life work. You want something different; you want something better; you want something more. I give you my commitment to provide you with the most beneficial knowledge that I have received, which enabled me to go from welfare to millionaire in one year.

But please don't believe a word I say. Got any idea why I would tell you that after you just spent twenty-some dollars for this *manual*?

I say it because all I can do, all any of us can do, is share what we know, and live.

I can feel some of you wiggling. "Oh God, what is this? I've got enough experience of my own. I could be getting some work done, or at least watching TV." So let me start by sharing with you the three most dangerous words in the English language. Got any ideas? They are:

I know that

Why would that be so bad? You know a lot of stuff. When you responded "Yes" to my two enrolling questions, you placed your foot on the path toward something. "I know that" stops you dead in your tracks.

Why?

Because when we think we know something, we shut down. We turn our attention off. We don't receive what is being offered to us. And I gave you my commitment that you are going to begin receiving more of everything you desire. So the first step is to disable the parts of you that hinder, block, or obstruct the expression of the intentions you have now set for yourself.

Yes, you say, but I do know many things.

Do you really?

Knowing is living. If your life is not a moment-to-moment practice of the things you say you know, then you don't *really* know it; you simply . . .

Read it—

Can recite it—

Saw it on TV—

Knowing is a profound experience beyond words.

I am writing this book because, twelve years ago, I thought I knew it all. In fact, I had achieved the highest dreams I'd set for myself. I had just won the Tony award and every other award Broadway has to offer; I had a beautiful mansion, two beautiful children, a great body; a marriage to a man I loved; and a career that showed signs of heading to the outposts of the universe. I had it all—or so I thought.

Boom! Within four months, it started to crumble; within three years, I had nothing. I was virtually a homeless single mom struggling to find work and depending on welfare to survive. I have wallowed in bitterness, self-hatred, and blame. I got so sick of myself that I went to see a psychiatrist to help me change my thinking, because I knew I was stuck. You know what happened?

The therapist, bless her, told me she could not help me. She told me my problems were not in my head but in the "real world." She told me I needed lawyers and accountants and business managers to solve my woes.

She was wrong.

You see, I had already spent years and my entire fortune doing exactly what she suggested. I had tried depending on others for help with my problems. But the dragon grew bigger and breathed harder down my neck.

I fell apart, and my life came together.

I spent the next seven years studying with the most dynamic educators on the planet. I spent those years using my life as the laboratory for what does and does not work for me—and in the process, I learned some laws that work for everyone.

I am asking for your commitment to get 1,000 percent out of what I am gifting to you. In order to do that, you need to suspend your "I know that" response, and instead, bring your attention right here and now. You need to open up, when it has been your habit to shut down.

Yes, or Yes?

Are you willing to do that?

Good, because . . .

How you do anything is how you do everything.

T. Harv Eker taught me that.

If you were unable to give a "Yes, or Yes" commitment, note that, and note exactly what your response is. In fact, write it down:

_____

_____

_____

Maybe you wrote, "I know that."

Or "I don't have time for that."

Perhaps, "I'm not in the mood."

Or "I'll come back to this later."

Whatever came up for you, now you have a record of something you "know."

You probably don't have time to get around to that high school or college degree that will take you to the next level, or you're not in the mood to make that important phone call—whatever it is you wrote down.

Because now you know one thing that takes you out of your happiness, out of your love, and out of receiving more of everything that you want. Maybe you're thinking, "But I don't use that excuse in my real life. I just wrote it down because I'm reading a book now."

I've got news for you. If it pops up in your head right now, it comes up everywhere. Because while you're reading this book, *this is your real life!* This is just a change of scenery. You are the same actor on the same stage.

Get over yourself—your time, your problems, your drama—and allow the life you were created for to manifest.

So let's get started. I'd like you to complete the questionnaires that follow. Write your answers down right on the pages. If you need extras, feel free to make photocopies.

■ SUCCESS ASSOCIATIONS EXERCISE ■

1. Success is _____

2. Success is _____

3. Success is _____

4. Money is _____

5. Money is _____

6. Financial freedom is _____

7. Celebrities are _____

8. The reasons I cannot or may not become successful are
   (List several) _____
   _____
   _____
   _____

9. Some of the possible negatives about being wealthy or going through
   the process of trying to become successful are
   (List several) _____

_____

_____

_____

10. My greatest worries and fears about becoming successful are
    (List several) _____

    _____

    _____

    _____

11. The worst thing about being wealthy is

    _____

    _____

    _____

■ BELIEF QUESTIONNAIRE ■

Rate your opinion with the numbers from 1 to 10 with regard to each of the following statements.

   1 means total disagreement; 10 means total agreement.

_____ 1. Money corrupts people.

_____ 2. Plan for the worst, but hope for the best.

_____ 3. I have to suffer for my art.

_____ 4. If I get psychologically healthy, I'll lose my edge.

_____ 5. Everyone has to pay their dues.

_____ 6. There is no such thing as overnight success.

_____ 7. You have to sleep your way to the top.

_____ 8. It's not what you know; it's whom you know.

_____ 9. I don't like selling or promoting.

_____10. If you're good, you'll be "discovered."

_____11. You've got to have something to fall back on.

_____12. The "Greats" die unappreciated.

_____13. I'll believe it when I see it.

_____14. I'm not good with money.

_____15. I'm getting this degree/certificate in case things don't work out in my chosen profession.

_____16. I have to give my art, my work, away to make connections.

_____17. I have to keep studying my entire life in order to be great.

_____18. Success is a matter of luck.

_____19. I don't want to be rich or famous.

_____20. I don't know what I would do if I fail.

_____21. Superstars are usually mediocre talents.

_____22. I'll try this out for a couple of years and if it doesn't work out, I'll try something else.

_____23. I need to be liked.

_____24. You can't fight fate.

_____25. I don't enjoy my work without praise from others.

_____26. Really talented people are always successful.

_____27. Some people are just born lucky.

_____28. The rich get richer, while the poor stumble along until they die.

_____29. I don't have enough education to do what I dream of.

_____30. There are no overnight successes.

_____31. I don't want the hassle of fame or fortune.

_____32. Women have a much harder time getting ahead.

_____33. Most rich people are miserable.

_____34. You've got to have money to get more.

_____35. I don't have to manage my money because I don't have any.

_____36. My chances of getting rich are slim to none.

_____37. If I get rich or successful, I'll lose my friends.

_____38. If I get rich, everybody will be begging me for something.

_____39. Why should I be rich when so many are starving?

_____40. People get rich by climbing over the backs of others.

_____41. I'm not good with money.

You are working in the laboratory of your life. You are the scientist collecting data. One of the things you don't know is yourself, but you've got a really good mirror. How often do you look into it to see yourself? How much of what you know about yourself comes from descriptions from your parents, siblings, teachers, or friends? Have you ever taken the time to find out if these descriptions were right? Well, you're going to do that now.

Whatever response you have to this present moment and everything in it reflects what you are doing/being/having, or it reflects what you are refusing to allow yourself to do/be/have.

EVERYTHING IN YOUR WORLD IS A MIRROR OF YOU.

Paul was always attracted to artistic types. He could spot their talent in an instant. He believed in them and encouraged them while he trudged through his days as an accountant, feeling that the world he loved was not open to him except through his connections to others. When he came to me for help, I asked him about his own artistic talents. At first he shrank, almost visibly, and said he had none. I wasn't giving up. "None? Not even a shred?" After a bit more prodding, Paul admitted that he had "an old hobby" of restoring and painting antique furniture.

"Why haven't you turned that into a thriving business, just as you have helped others catapult their artistic endeavors into businesses that make their life's joy into their life's work?" Paul mumbled that there was "no money in it."

I suggested he spend some time compiling a list of stores and prices for hand-painted antiques ("numbers don't lie" means something to any accountant). After all, someone was indeed making money out there with an "old hobby" like his—he couldn't deny that. But the next thing he said was that he didn't have the artistic temperament.

I wasn't taking that for an answer. "Paul, the talents that you enjoy in your clients—it's what your own artistic temperament is seeking." We worked on his realizing that, believing that, and really feeling that. Soon he realized that the creative talent he had seen so clearly in others was the reflection of his own abilities.

The Talmud says, *"We do not see things as they are. We see things as we are."*

Margo wanted to quit her job. She hated being an attorney; she hated everyone at her law office; she even felt she hated most of her clients. She told me this feeling had been building for several years, during which time she had given up her daily running regimen and put on thirty pounds. She no longer had time to do volunteer work for the children's aid organization, either.

I asked Margo if she was sure it was really her job she hated. Perhaps she was hating herself. "Yes!" she wailed. "I hate taking on more and more clients and having less and less time for me. I used to feel good and look great. I used to help people. Now I'm just a corporate whore!" And then it hit her: The work hadn't changed, the clients hadn't changed; *she* had changed, and she was projecting her change onto her world. She had stopped taking care of herself. She had stopped maintaining her priorities. "The sad part," she added, "is that nobody even asked me to. I simply volunteered myself into corporate slavery, but I guess I can volunteer myself back out."

And that's exactly what she did. Now she's a partner. She doesn't hate her work; she's running, feeling fit again, and volunteering her time. She didn't have to change her profession; she had to change herself.

Margo had to give up the drama of her oppressive job in order to create the reality of the life deserved. What do you have to give up?

This is not your cue to wallow in harsh self-judgment or criticism as you glimpse yourself in these examples. This is your moment to shine in the light of awareness, for it's what we don't know that we don't know about ourselves that does us in.

To know that we know what we know, and to know that we do
not know what we do not know, that is true knowledge.

—Copernicus

You're here to *un*learn, and in the process, to find out what you already know, and then expand upon it. Are you thinking, "I'll believe it when I see it"? Isn't that what you were taught—to believe what you see? But you don't, really, because if you did, you would understand everything that is in your own life.

Instead of believing it when you see it, I say that you won't *see* it until you *believe* it.

What if you genuinely believed, "I deserve to be rich, successful, (substitute your own desire), because I add value to other people's lives"?

I bet that's what Deepak Chopra, Bill Gates, Oprah Winfrey, and thousands of other wealthy, successful people believe, and whether or not you think so right now, you can too.

Right now.

Stand up. Place your hand over your heart and speak loudly, affirming:

> *I give up all the stories*
> *that hold me back*
> *and I embrace the infinite potential*
> *that is mine to express.*

Feel that resonate in your chest, in your bones.

Now say it again, louder.

Now check in with yourself. Do you feel vibrant and alive, or somehow false? Prideful and arrogant?

EVENTS HAVE THE MEANING YOU GIVE THEM.

What new story are you telling yourself, after speaking a single supportive statement? Note this story and the feeling, whatever it is. Write it down. Why? Because then it's a set of facts. Byron Katie, founder of a program called The Work, noted that when you think or say something, the minute someone calls you on it, you can wriggle out, saying, "That's not what I meant" or "You misunderstood me." But when you write it down, it's concrete. It is what it is. And if it's what first came up, it's probably "your truth." So write it down.

_____

_____

_____

_____

_____

This is what keeps you from your power and your glory, and keeps you locked in a world created by what you have been told, what you have heard or seen.

Genius is self-bestowed; mediocrity is self-afflicted.

—Walter Russell, scientist,
philosopher, composer, athlete,
architect, artist, and inventor

Successful people live beyond what already is in their world. They live beyond their own histories. They don't just rearrange the old; they call things into existence from beyond the veil of the invisible.

What lies behind the veil for you?

That famous philosopher Anonymous once said that you are never given a dream without being given the ability to achieve it. Anonymous also said that if you can conceive it, you can achieve it, because the very ability to think something up implies that the mechanism for its manifestation already exists in the universe. One has only to be a receptive and willing vessel for the revelation of that information.

There's a story of a man who died and was whisked up to Heaven. On one side of the gate was a room filled from floor to ceiling with gifts. Sitting in the middle of the room was what appeared to be a doorman with his head hanging low, looking most distressed. The man asked him, "What's wrong? You're in this room with all these gifts—what are they for?" The doorman replied, "Oh, these are all the dreams people gave up on before we got a chance to deliver them."

What dream have you given up on?

Thomas Alva Edison, born into poverty, was said to have failed over a thousand times in his attempts to create the incandescent light. Someone asked how he continued to believe the lightbulb was even possible. He replied: "Those were steps on my way. In each attempt I was successful in finding a way *not* to create a lightbulb. I was always eager to learn, even from my mistakes."

So one thing most of us know a lot about is the ways *not* to be wealthy, *not* to be happy, *not* to be successful. If we thought like Edison, we'd be well on our way to wealth, happiness, success, and much, much more.

Edison did not invent electricity. It was in existence, of course, in its fullness, when the pharaohs walked the planet. What Edison did was to ask a question, and then stay open and willing to endure a thousand failures with the faith that, in time, the answer would be revealed.

What question have you been asking?

How can I pay my bills? How can I make it through another day?

The size of the question determines the size of the answer.

Ask bigger!

Turn on the light.

Are you willing to endure failure in eager expectation that your heart's desire will, and must, be fulfilled?

Yes, or Yes?

Are you willing to learn from your mistakes, or do you always have a reason why it didn't work out? Do you live above the line or below it?

Most of us live below the line in

$$\frac{\quad\quad\quad}{\text{BLAME}}$$

However, if we would live above the line:

$$\frac{\text{LEARN}}{\text{BLAME}}$$

If we would learn from our every mistake, we could move a step closer to fulfilling our highest desires.

You have a lot of experience. You know a lot of things that you don't even know you know. Let's begin to discover what you know.

Are you willing to allow every moment of your life to reveal the stepping-stone to the next great adventure?

Yes, or Yes?

Then let's get started.

You are going to write down your life exactly as you see it now, in every detail of every area of it: home, family, love, health, body, sex, finances, career, happiness, friendship, religion, ambition, fulfillment.

In each category, I will write an example of how the story can go, and then you will write your own story.

HOME. · Example: "I have a beautiful house in a great neighborhood. I love to wake up there every day. If I died there, I'd be happy." Another example: "I'm living with friends because I haven't been able to afford my own place." Or, "because I can't figure out where I want to live." Or whatever your story may be.

MY HOME:

_____

_____

_____

_____

_____

_____

_____

FAMILY. · Example: "My family has been supportive of everything I ever wanted." Another example: "I don't have a family. My parents died and I never married." Or, "My partner and kids are why I do what I do." Or "I haven't talked to those folks in years; my friends are my family." Or whatever your story is. Please write about both your family of origin and the family you may have created.

MY FAMILY:

_____

_____

_____

_____

_____

_____

_____

_____

LOVE. · Example: "I have a wonderful relationship with a loving partner whom I've been with for years. We respect each other." Another example: "It hasn't worked out with anyone just yet. Still, I'm hopeful." Or "I like being with me."

MY LOVE LIFE:

BODY. · Example: "I'm a little overweight. I joined a gym. I'm working on it." Another example: "I'm not feeling too great. I'm too tired to exercise." Or "I'm in great shape. I'm very athletic. I love to move around a lot, and I exercise every day."

MY BODY:

_____

_____

_____

_____

_____

_____

HEALTH. · Example: "My health is good. I haven't needed to see a doctor in years." Another example: "I have so many allergies, I suffer constantly. I'm out of work a few weeks a year." Or "I can barely get out of bed; the doctor says I shouldn't even be working."

MY HEALTH:

_____

_____

_____

_____

_____

_____

SEX. · Example: "I enjoy sex, and I experience it often." Another example: "It's been about ten years. I was really hurt." Or "Sex has never been very important to me."

MY SEX LIFE:

_____

_____

_____

_____

_____

_____

_____

FINANCES. · Example: "I am financially free." Another example: "I'm constantly robbing Peter to pay Paul. I work two jobs; I don't know how else to make ends meet, but it's never enough." Or "I work hard and I pay my bills. I don't have anything left over, but I have everything I want." Or "I'm living off credit cards."

MY FINANCES:

_____

_____

_____

_____

_____

_____

_____

CAREER. · Example: "I hate my job, but it pays the bills." Another example: "I'm in a beginning position and I'm primed to move up." Or "I have a vision of the career I desire, and I'm making the connections to make it happen."

MY CAREER:

_____

_____

_____

_____

_____

HAPPINESS. · Example: "It's overrated. I have a job, a family, I'm secure, that's enough." Another example: "Sometimes I'm happy, but then
something will happen and I crash." Or "Happiness? I wish I knew what
that was."

MY TAKE ON HAPPINESS:

_____

_____

_____

_____

_____

_____

_____

FRIENDSHIP. · Example: "I'm still friends with my best friend from
grammar school, whom I would trust with my life." Another example:
"I've got a couple of friends, but I'm basically a loner. I don't like other
people getting into my business." Or, "I'm so busy with work and family
that there's no time for socializing."

MY FRIENDSHIPS:

_____

_____

_____

_____

_____

RELIGION/SPIRITUALITY. · Example: "I think anybody who buys
into organized religion is an idiot." Another example: "I have an active
spiritual life, but no particular religion. I attend a variety of services." Or
"No time, no time, no time. And I don't need it."

MY RELIGIOUS/SPIRITUAL LIFE:

_____

_____

_____

_____

_____

What we have just done is an inventory of your fruits. And fruits come from roots.

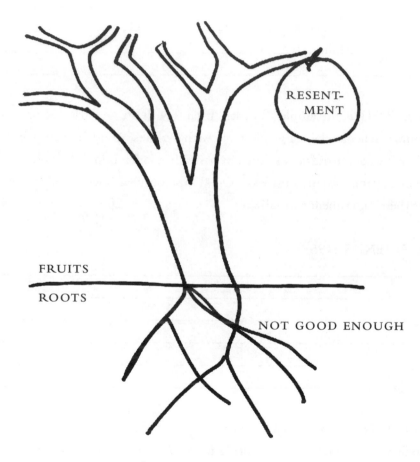

If you have disease in the roots, it cannot help but pass up into the fruits.

Bill was an emergency medical service worker. He'd been doing it for years, and he told me he loved his job. He made a decent salary, but somehow he never had any money left over. He planned to save, but some emergency always came up that required him to spend everything he had.

I asked Bill how he felt about having money, and he shrugged. "You want to have it or you don't want to have it?" I asked. "It's not life and death," he replied.

But it was life and death for Bill.

You see, when Bill was a teenager, he had taken a CPR course as one of his high school requirements. He told me his parents were always fighting about money in those days. One day over dinner, while his mom and dad were engaged in a heated argument, his father choked. Bill anxiously tried out his CPR techniques, but his father died in his arms.

I asked Bill if he thought that incident might have anything to do with his inability to hang on to money and possibly even with his chosen profession. He wasn't sure. What I showed him was that this incident had created a negative root where money was concerned. Bill could make money but he couldn't keep it because he associated it with his father's death.

Or take Janet, a successful entrepreneur of several small businesses. As soon as she got them up and running well, however, she'd want out. The profitable businesses didn't hold any interest for her. This had become a pattern in her life. She'd create successes only to walk away before she even realized how far they could go.

Janet's pattern represents what Robert Fritz, in his book *Creating*, calls "rubber band." Fritz says most people spend their lives moving between two poles attached by an imaginary rubber band. When pressure builds up at one pole and a situation becomes uncomfortable, these people move to the second pole, away from the first, creating distance from the difficult situation.

Some of us use food, sex, work, or any number of activities or inactivity to get away from a bad situation.

As the stressful pole recedes, we experience relief from the situation, and when we no longer feel the pressure, we stop the action. Then, however, the rubber band springs back, leaving us in the same—and sometimes an even worse—situation, from which we continue to move away, only to continue falling back.

It turns out that Janet was a middle child, and her parents never expected much of her. All their hopes were on her older brother, who hadn't amounted to much, and her younger sister, who was a happy housewife. All her life, Janet had been told she'd never succeed. So what do you think her root for success was?

Janet's success was fueled by the pressure to prove her parents wrong. She was moving away from their disapproval, but as soon as she created a success, her resentment at having to do so in the first place would rise, and she would relapse to where she began. She repeated this again and again. In a later chapter, I will teach you some processes to dilute or even remove negative roots. For now, think about what some of your roots are.

Is home, family, love, health, body, sex, finances, career, happiness, friendship, or religion tied up with a negative root—that is, when you seek these things, is it only to get away from something else? If that is the case, you will always relapse. In fact, the only way to break out of this cycle is to stop moving *away from* what you do not want and to begin moving *toward* what you do want.

There is nothing in the outside world that needs to be different. Your partner doesn't have to change; your body doesn't have to change. In many African villages in the midst of war-torn countries with limited access to good food and water, people have been able to create good food and water resources for their villages. They didn't stop the war or change the country, but in their arena they created what they wanted and needed.

What I know from my life is that many of the dragons that first knocked me down are still there, but because I changed my thinking, I began moving toward what I wanted, rather than away from what was terrorizing me. The psychiatrist was wrong: My problems were not in the real world, because every one of those problems still existed when I wrote this book, but my life is night-and-day different from what it was back then, and all because I stopped looking "over there" and started looking inside of me.

That's what you've just been doing right now. Because of this work I have created a beautiful life for my children and myself, and you can do that too.

Are you ready to change your thinking and thus change your life?

Yes, or Yes?

Then it is already done. It has only to unfold in time.

| ONE: REVIEW |

Studies show that review is an essential key to learning. In all accelerated learning techniques, review is built in. Learning requires review just as a lightbulb needs a switch, because—

What I *see*,

I *forget*.

What I hear,

I *remember*.

But what I do,

I *understand*!

The purpose of this book is not for you to see my words and diagrams and mentally hear the thoughts and ideas, but to actually engage in processes that will change your life. They really do work.

The redundancy, the open questions, are all part of proven processes that reeducate people from the cellular level. Research shows that material is retained best in memory, and its impact and usefulness to the student are maximized, if it is reviewed three times: once within ten hours after being taught, again twenty-four hours later, and a third time seven days later. Information taught once and not reviewed at all can become virtually impossible to retain in memory or put to good use.

At the end of each chapter is a cumulative review of all of the previous chapters. Pick up the review often to retain the material so that you can make changes in your behavior, and hence in your life.

1. I K T
   I know that

2. How you do anything is _____.

3. You'll see it when _____.

4. Events have the meaning_____.

5. Genius is _____, while Mediocrity is

   _____.

6.   L _____

                            B

7. Diagram of the tree with roots.

8. What I *see*, I *forget*.
   What I *hear*, I *remember*.
   But what I DO, I *understand*.

TWO

DISCOVER WHAT
YOU REALLY WANT

If I can show you how you got where you are, would you be interested in that? If I can show you how to change the course of your future, would you be interested in that?

Good, because

$$T \rightarrow F \rightarrow A$$

Thoughts lead to Feelings, which produce Action.

Let's say you wake up and hear the rain outside your window and your first thought is "Damn, it's gonna be a miserable rainy day!" Do you feel good about that? No. You already have the headache or the arthritis. You don't want to leave the house. So you drag yourself out of bed and stub your toe. You curse, confirming your original thought. You look in the cupboard and your favorite cereal is gone. You go to get dressed, and your suit or dress has a stain on it. Every moment confirms that feeling, which began with the original negative thought. You arrive at work and your boss comes into your cubicle, and you turn away and cringe because your clothes are stained. She wants you to start a new project, but the way you're behaving might lead her to change her mind. Or she asks you anyway. Are you going to be excited and ready to do what needs to be done? Probably not. You might even choose to avoid or postpone it until a better day. Your mood and your actions will reflect that original negative thought, resulting in a day where nothing gets accomplished.

But let's say you wake up and hear the rain on the windowsill and your first thought is, "I'm getting a blessing today." What does that make you feel? Excitement, anticipation: Something great is out there waiting for you. You jump out of that bed so quickly you stub your toe. You think, "Thank you for the reminder to move this dresser right now so this never happens again!" You move the dresser and feel relieved. Then you go into the kitchen, but your favorite cereal is gone. So you pick that year-old box of oatmeal instead, and vow to start that health regimen you've been thinking about for so long. You go to the closet and discover that your outfit has a stain on it, so you pull out that other outfit someone gave you and you weren't too sure about. Now, because you have no other alternative, you trust that it will work out fine. You get to work, and the boss comes in and compliments you on your new look. You sit up a little taller. He tells you he has a new project for you to work on. Are you cringing to avoid it? Or is this the confirmation of the thought you had when you first woke up? Didn't you feel something good coming your way—and now you're ready to do it, and do it well.

Everything that has ever existed began as a thought. Before the chair you are sitting in was made, someone had a thought about the design for it, and then they drew it or shared the idea with someone else, until they came up with a form that came as close to their thought as possible. This is the act of creation.

Fortunately, or unfortunately, this process is automatic. Each of us unconsciously thinks all day. Every one of those thoughts produces a feeling that leads to an action, thousands of times each day. In thousands of moments and decisions a day, this exact process is unbroken:

Thought → Feeling → Action.

How many thoughts are your own? How many are foisted upon you by images in newspapers, on TV screens, sounds from the radio, neighbors, passing cars? You are affected by everyone and everything. Unless you consciously become aware of this fact, you continue to go through your life reacting to events and circumstances, and wondering how they came to be.

Most of the time it's not you thinking the thoughts, but it's the thoughts that are thinking you. Doubt it? Just try to stop it for even one minute. It's impossible. And yet this is the process by which everything that is in your life has come to be there. If you want to know what you think, feel, and do—look at what you've got.

Let's look at the Life Map that we did in Chapter 1. Now we are going to rewrite it, in order to find out what we really believe.

For the next exercise, you can use a separate piece of paper, or you can write in this book. You are going to rewrite each of the categories: home, family, love, health, body, sex, financial condition, career, happiness, friendship, religion; this time, writing each as an "I believe" statement. If what you wrote is supportive, you will rewrite it as, "I believe that I can . . ." If the statement is not supportive, you will rewrite it as, "I believe that I cannot . . ."

FAMILY: · Example: "I believe that I can have a family that supports me in everything I have ever wanted to accomplish." Or, "I believe that I cannot have a supportive family, and I believe that my partner and kids are why I do what I do." Or, "I believe that I cannot talk to my folks. I believe that my friends are my family."

I believe:

_____

_____

_____

_____

_____

_____

LOVE: · Example: "I believe that I can have a wonderful relationship with a loving partner that can last for years, and we can respect each other." Or, "I believe that it can't work out with anyone. I believe that I can hope, but it will probably never happen." Or, "I believe that I must really like being alone."

I believe:

_____

_____

_____

_____

_____

_____

_____

BODY: · Example: "I believe that I can defeat being overweight. I believe I'm working on it by joining the gym." Or, "I believe that I cannot reach the point where I feel great about myself physically. I believe that I can't find the time to change what's wrong." Or, "I believe that I can be in great shape. I believe that I can be very athletic and energetic. I believe that I can love moving every day."

I believe:

_____

_____

_____

_____

_____

_____

_____

HEALTH: · Example: "I believe that I can be healthy and feel great. I believe that I can be so healthy I won't need to see a doctor for years." Or, "I believe that I can never be allergy-free. I believe that I just cannot ever have a good immune system." Or, "I believe that I can't get out of bed. I believe that I can't even work."

I believe:

_____

_____

_____

_____

_____

_____

SEX: · Example: "I believe that I can be sexy. I believe that I can enjoy sex and have it often." Or, "I believe that I cannot get with the sex thing, and that's why I haven't had it for years. I believe this because I was really hurt last time around." Or, "I believe that I can't begin to care about sex because it's never been important to me."

I believe:

_____

_____

_____

_____

_____

_____

FINANCES: · Example: "I believe that I can be financially free." Or, "I believe that there's no way out for me; all I can do is rob Peter to pay Paul. I believe that I can't get by without working two jobs. I believe that I can't make ends meet. I believe that I can't ever make enough. I believe that something always has to come up to drain my resources and prevent me from saving." Or, "I believe that I can't live day to day except on credit cards."

I believe:

_____

_____

_____

_____

_____

_____

CAREER: · Example: "I believe that I can't have a job that pays more than just the bills." Or, "I believe that I can start at the bottom and move on up." Or, "I believe that I can envision the career I want, and I can make the connections to make it happen."

I believe:

_____

_____

_____

_____

_____

_____

HAPPINESS: · Example: "I believe that happiness is overrated. If I can have a job, family, and a bit of security, I can't ask for anything more." Or, "I believe that I cannot be happy without something happening to make me crash." Or, "I believe that I cannot ever know what happiness is."

I believe:

_____

_____

_____

_____

_____

FRIENDSHIP: · Example: "I believe that I can have best friends for life. I believe that I can trust them completely." Or, "I believe that I cannot have more than a couple of friends. I believe that I'm a loner. I believe that I can't have friends without them getting into my business." Or, "I believe that I can't have friends and still fulfill my obligations to work and family."

I believe:

_____

_____

_____

_____

_____

_____

RELIGION: · Example: "I believe that I can't take part in organized religion without being an idiot." Or, "I believe that I can have an active spiritual life. I believe that I can attend a variety of religious services and get support and benefit from them." Or, "I believe that I can't make the time or really feel the need for religion."

I believe:

_____

_____

_____

_____

_____

_____

You have just made an inventory of your fruits. Is it a harvest or blight? Do you want to continue to reap these crops year after year? Maybe you didn't even know what you had planted. Maybe somebody else planted those seeds. But this is your life. You can't argue with the fruits; they grow naturally from the seeds.

Argue with reality, and you lose, but only 100% of the time.

—Byron Katie

Everything you have in your life is a function of your past actions. And every action you have taken is a function of what you believe. It began as a thought, which produced a feeling, which led to an action.

Maybe you don't think you believe some of the things you have written. Do you know where you might have heard, seen, or picked up such ideas? Was it from parents, friends, teachers, TV? Did you ever stop to notice that you were running programs that didn't match your current belief system? Yet your actions are still following the old operating system. Some of these programs were installed years, even decades ago; some were installed by people you don't even respect.

You know, you clean out your garage, your closet, your desk, but how often do you clean out your mind? How often do you go in and check to make sure the operating system you're currently running is up to speed with the programs you want to play today? Not very often.

We learn from what we see, what we hear, and what is modeled for us. And we can unlearn, and choose to learn, by those same methods.

Lisa Kron wrote an autobiographical play about her family, entitled *WELL.* In that play, she explores her family's culture of illness, and how she somehow broke free from that environment.

You, too, can break free of the stories you've been living. You can change the operating systems you run by installing new software. But not until you have carefully examined where you were.

I'm sure that some of what you see shocks you. No one could have convinced you that you really believed such things. But there are the fruits; now you know. You couldn't do anything about changing the fruits until you knew they were there, because it isn't true that "what you don't know won't hurt you." Not knowing enough about yourself can hurt you a lot. Not understanding how your beliefs can hold you back from your desires can do you in.

Now, I'm not talking about random thoughts that drop in at a fast rate

during your day. You can't prevent negative impressions that naturally occur when there are negative stimuli. Just reading the newspaper takes you
on a roller-coaster ride of emotion. How do you usually feel after reading
the paper? I know I feel like the world is not a great place, and I need to
work hard to remind myself how wonderful it really is.

If you want to change what you've got, you're going to have to work
that hard, too.

In 1993, when I was at the apex of my career, I lost custody of my two
little boys, then three and six years old, in a bruising court battle. Still reeling, I had to face the continued litigation that spanned the next twelve
years of my life, gobbling up my financial resources and leaving me with
the feeling that not only was there no justice, but that the government and
all of its agencies would never help. And let me tell you, I had the evidence
to prove it. A film company even wanted to make a movie about the trav-
esty of my experience in the court system.

When I began doing this mental work, I learned that my experience of
injustice, and the lack of government accountability and responsibility, had
a root in my own thoughts and feelings of abuse and betrayal by the system.
And I had the stories to prove it. It could have been a miniseries.

You know what happened? I asked myself this question: Could my belief in the ineffectiveness of government systems be creating that as my reality? If the injustice was "real," my thought about it should not have
changed the reality of it. So I decided to give myself a new thought, and I
practiced saying it and feeling it. The thought was that government systems and agencies can really provide me with useful services. They can help
me; they *will* help me.

Very soon after I began this practice, I met a woman in the park who
was on welfare. She told me, however, that the Department of Social Services was paying for her child to go to a *private school*. This program had not
just started the day after I set my mind to thinking differently; it had been
going on long before that. But my negative belief about government agencies had placed a screen around my mind, which filtered out all information

contrary to the belief I already held. When I decided to think differently (and I had no tangible reason to do so, other than my faith that these principles are impersonal laws that work for everyone), suddenly the world changed. Now I saw it this way: The government could put my kids through school and pay my child care expenses so I could get a job. Had the world really changed, or had I changed?

There is no reality in the absence of observation.
— The Copenhagen Interpretation of Quantum Mechanics

In other words, the answer to the age-old question "If a tree falls in the forest and there is no one there to hear it, does it make a sound?" is—*no*. Because in the absence of an observer, there is no tree and no forest.

You and I call worlds into reality by our every thought, worlds that do not exist until we think them into being.

No, no—you're not buying it.

And I bet for every story in your inventory you've got a cause, a reason. In his book *Wisdom from an Empty Mind,* Jacob Liberman poses this question: "Who would you be if you woke up tomorrow with amnesia? Would you still have that arthritic pain, would the effects of your diagnosis still remain? Or does the diagnosis create the symptom and the pain?"

Stay with me. What if you let go of your story? "I'm this way because my mother . . ." or "my father . . ." or "my wife . . ." or "my husband . . ."? What if you let the story go?

You don't want to, do you? What's your resistance made of? Write down the reasons why you don't want to believe this.

_____

_____

_____

_____

_____

Whatever you wrote is what you sacrifice your happiness to. And I wager that it fits into one of the following categories, because most people will give up their joy, their freedom, and their happiness in order to:

1. Prove somebody wrong;
2. Prove themselves right;
3. Keep someone from hurting them;
4. Hurt someone for having hurt them;
5. Prove how good they are; or
6. Prove how bad someone else is.

Which category does your story fall into?

Your story only reflects how you choose to see the events in your past. Events are impersonal. But most of us don't see reality; we see our interpretations of reality.

Brenna knew her mother didn't like her. She felt it from the time she was a small child. I asked her what made her feel this, and she related an incident where her mother had tried to kill her. She remembered lying on the bed with her mother choking her. She couldn't remember how it ended, but from that moment on, she knew her mother hated her. Brenna was a fifty-year-old woman who had missed many a moment with her mother because of this story. She was committed to it, and had amassed a dozen other stories about her mother to confirm it. But the ultimate effect of this story in Brenna's own life was that she was unable to relate lovingly to her own daughter. She said, "I don't know how; I'm afraid I'll hurt her the way my mother hurt me." I asked her if she was willing to let the story go. And by let the story go, I meant: (a) to never tell the story again, and (b) to remanufacture the story as she would have liked it.

Brenna resisted: "I can't erase the fact that she choked me. She tried to kill me!" She became hysterical even speaking about it. I suggested that before she went to bed that night, she should try to "see" a different story, the story of her dream.

I ask you now to take one of your less supportive circumstances, and re-create the story of how it came to be. For instance, take "I can't handle money because my family never had any," and turn it into, "I am a great money manager because my family never had any money."

Here is a story of two sisters, one of whom grew up to be a very unhappy, miserable woman, abusive to her children. Asked why she was so angry and abusive, she said, "Because my father was always angry and abusive to me." Her sister had grown up to be a very happy, gentle, and pleasant woman, a loving mother to her family. Asked how she turned out that way, she replied, "Because my father was always so angry and abusive to me."

The events were the same, but the thoughts, feelings, and actions about the event made the critical difference in these two women's lives.

You get to choose. You might not be able to choose the "facts," but you can choose your responses. And it doesn't matter that you're in the middle of the river of your life; there are no time, place, or age requirements. You can choose to change the story right now.

Are you willing to do that?

Or would you rather be right than move forward in your life?

As it turns out, Brenna was ultimately willing to try my idea. As ridiculous as she thought it was, she was willing to make up a story about her wonderful relationship with her mother. When friends complained about their mothers, she bit her tongue and withheld her own stories. She confided in me that although she couldn't believe it, it felt as if her mother had also become a new person. She was kinder and gentler, more loving toward Brenna. In fact, they became so much closer that one day Brenna felt comfortable enough to ask her mother about the choking incident. "The look on my mother's face was horrifying," Brenna said. "How she cried! She asked me, 'You really believed that about me? You don't remember jumping on the bed and eating a piece of candy, and it getting caught in your throat? I love you! I threw you on the bed to pry that candy out of your throat to save your life!'"

Two lives were changed forever, all because one person was willing to give up her story. Brenna was willing to risk being wrong for the sake of being happy, and for her, it worked.

I have witnessed men and women finding the blessing in all kinds of loss and grief. There is a blessing in the life you are living right now. Schopenhauer said that if you look at a person's life backward, it turns out to be a perfect road map to exactly where they end up.

There are no accidents or mistakes. You are reading this manual because you are ready to take notice of the signs, rather than to continue to be blindly driven through life as if at the mercy of historical events, peoples, and things beyond your control.

Reread your inventory and replace the words "I believe" with "I think," "I feel," "I act."

Your life is what you know. It is a perfect reflection or road map of every thought, feeling, and action you have ever had. If you want to change what the reflection or the map looks like, where do you begin?

You begin with the thought.

I know that thought is the root of all manifestation. I want you to know it too. So let's work with a thought. Go to the success and belief questionnaires on pages 7–9 and circle the belief statements with the highest numbers. Circle the eights, nines, and tens. In case you hadn't noticed, almost everything on the list is a nonsupportive thought or belief. Now choose just one of those high-number beliefs to work with. Write it down.

_____

_____

_____

Now rewrite it in a positive form. If you wrote, "The rich get richer while the poor stumble along until they die," change it to something like, "The rich get richer, and so can I." If you wrote, "I don't have enough education to do what I dream," change it to, "I have more than enough education to do whatever I dream." Do it now.

_____

_____

Chances are you have resistance to this new story. Write it down.

_____

_____

_____

_____

The more you know about how you think right now, the better equipped you'll be to rethink yourself into the life you desire.

All that we are is the result of what we have thought.
The mind is everything.
What we think, we become.

—Maharishi Yogi

Now take the top five beliefs—the ones with the highest numbers—and write them in the chart below. For each thought, you are going to write the feeling that goes with it, and for each feeling, you are going to write the percentage or degree of you that feels that way.

For example:

THOUGHT	FEELING	DEGREE OF FEELING
Most rich people are miserable.	Hopeless	80%

Now rewrite the thought in the positive form. Write the corresponding feeling and the degree of that feeling.

THOUGHT	FEELING	DEGREE OF FEELING
Most rich people are very happy.	Hopeful	30%

It doesn't matter if the degree of saturation of the new feeling is low. One candle can light a dark room. What matters is that we begin to light the candles to dispel the darkness that has filled our heart, mind, and spirit, the darkness that has created the very things we are trying to get away from. What matters is that we begin to create a space of light, and a place we want to move to.

Are you ready to create that space and light?

Remember that how you judge the world is how you judge yourself. And if you see something "over there," it's inside you too. Look: If we don't know a thing, we can't recognize it. If you didn't already know what is in this manual, you wouldn't hear it or recognize it even as you're reading it.

You're ready to wake up, and I'm here to remind you:

When you wake up tomorrow, let your first thought be the new version of the old nonsupportive belief. Place your hand on your heart and speak it before you get out of bed. Write it on a piece of paper and look at it throughout the day. Write it down several times.

Later we will delve deeply into the laws of manifestation. For now, use as many of your senses as possible to engage with your new thought. For the visual sense and tactile sense: Write it down. For the aural sense: speak it aloud.

Perhaps you recall from your physics class that light is both a particle and a wave. If no one is paying attention, it's everywhere and acts like a wave; but the minute you or I try to see it, it's in one place acting like a particle. Are you following me?

You and I, by our thought, intention, and decision, limit the infinite to one finite instance in space and time. But the reality for the light is that it's still everywhere; we just don't see it that way.

But what if you chose to wake up every day and call forth the thought of your highest infinite self? Are you ready to do that? Because that is the truth of your being. There is nothing impossible for you unless you think it so.

> The opposite of a fact is falsehood,
> but the opposite of one profound truth
> may very well be another profound truth.
>
> —Niels Bohr

So let's take it to the next level. Are you ready for that?

Take one of the beliefs from the questionnaire to which you gave a high number, and see if it still has a low level of saturation when you turned it into a positive belief. What we are looking for here is a belief you are so sure is the truth that we might just have to kill you to convince you otherwise.

You got something?

What follows next is a writing exercise that calls upon the depth of your humanity. Most of us would do more for another than we would do for ourselves. Unfortunately, we can only do for another what we really can do for ourselves. The good news is that we can do much more than we know.

So on the next page you will find a letter. Imagine that you have arrived home from a very stressful day at work or school or with the kids, only to find this letter pushed under your door. The envelope is blank.

There will be blank spaces in the letter. *Before you read the letter,* write the high-number belief you have chosen to work with in the blank spaces. In fact, write that belief again now.

_____

_____

_____

After you have filled in the blank spaces with your belief, read the letter.

Dear Best Friend (Lover, Parent, Child):

I know you will never forgive me for this, but I have decided to end my life. I wanted you to know that it is not your fault or responsibility. I accept complete responsibility for my decision, and I am only writing you to tell you I love you and to apologize for any ways I may have hurt you—but mostly to let you know that you were the most meaningful part of my life, and I thank you for being in it.

Unfortunately, I cannot bear living another day. I can never overcome the fact that _____

_____,

and I don't want to keep living in a world that's made that way. I have listened to everyone's advice and they are all wrong or it just doesn't apply to me. In my world, _____

_____.

And I can't take it any longer. I can't ever be what I want to be. I'm not lucky. Everyone else gets the breaks. Fortune has never smiled on me. I'm miserable, and I'm tired of making other people miserable.

You are the only one who ever listened. You are the only one who seemed to care. I didn't even appreciate all you did. My life is not worth living because _____

_____. I

will be dead by the time you read this, but just know there was nothing you could have done to stop me.

Good-bye,

Best Friend (Lover, Child, Parent)

How do you feel? Have you ever felt the way they felt? Do you know this kind of pain? If you could have reached them, what would you have been able to say? Could you think of anything to encourage them to go on? Can you tell them why the world is not the way their belief paints it?

Write it down:

————————————————————————————
————————————————————————————
————————————————————————————
————————————————————————————
————————————————————————————
————————————————————————————
————————————————————————————
————————————————————————————
————————————————————————————
————————————————————————————
————————————————————————————
————————————————————————————

Now imagine the phone ringing.

Your friend was found in time, but is in critical condition in a hospital, in a coma. You rush to the hospital and stand at the bedside and read them what you wrote.

Read it aloud now.

Were you able to come up with some reasons for that person to go on living? Were you able to tell them why that belief they held isn't always true?

What I added here were higher stakes. We can do anything if the stakes are high enough. If I asked you to raise a million dollars in the next month, you'd probably say it's impossible. But if your child's or parent's or partner's life depended on it, you'd have a different response; suddenly you would muster the energy to do the impossible.

Sometimes I've believed as many as six impossible things before breakfast.

—Lewis Carroll

When we are young, we expect to live forever. When we are older, we don't expect that anymore. In either instance, the stakes aren't high enough to motivate us out of the status quo.

Status quo thinking got us where we are today. Status quo thinking will keep us here. So we've got to up the stakes. Why is it important for you to be healthy, wealthy, and successful? Start thinking about it now, because until you know why it's important, and until the stakes are so high that the consequences of missing out are unacceptable, you will not have the impetus to move.

It begins with thought. If you think it's crucial to succeed, you will do it; if you think it's insignificant, you probably will not. So why not begin rethinking the stakes for your freedom, success, health, and happiness?

Take one thought from your list. Turn it around. Up the stakes for overcoming it. What thought did you choose? Write it down:

_____

Now rewrite the supportive version:

_____

What will happen if you don't overcome it?

_____

What will happen when you know it's not true?

_____

_____

_____

Work with this thought for one day, or one week, and watch the magic happen.

1. I K T

   I know that

2. How you do anything is _____.

3. You'll see it when _____.

4. Events have the meaning _____.

5. Genius is _____, while Mediocrity is

   _____ .

6.   L _____

                      B

7. Diagram of the tree with roots.

8. What I *see*, I *forget*.
   What I *hear*, I *remember*.
   But what I *do*, I *understand*.

9. T → F → A

   Thoughts lead to Feelings, which produce Action.

10. It's what you don't know that you don't _____ that does you in.

11. Prove somebody wrong?

    Prove themselves right?

    Keep someone from hurting them?

    Hurt someone for hurting them?

    Prove how good they are?

    Prove how bad someone else is?

12.

THOUGHT	FEELING	DEGREE OF FEELING
Most rich people are very happy.	Hopeful	30%

13. Upping the stakes

THREE

DE-INSTALL THE BUTTONS
THAT TAKE YOU OUT

If I can show you how to neutralize and/or de-install the buttons that take you out, would you be interested in that?

And if I can show you how to stop new buttons from being installed, would you be interested in that?

Good, because here is where we begin to rewrite history. Maybe you've heard that it can't be done, but it's done every day. History is written by the victors. You are about to claim victory over the stories and events that have limited you, so far, to what you are doing, being, and having right now.

We are accustomed to having access to information in the form of memories and knowledge of the present and past. We are accustomed to believing that our past and our present create our future.

Beginning with Einstein's theory of relativity, though, science began to say that space and time are not two separate things, but one single thing. If that is so, why should we have access to only two parts of the one thing—namely, the past and the present—instead of having access to all three parts of the one thing, which includes the future?

There is no answer to that question because there is no reason why not.

Imagine that you are standing outside, and you look down and see a rock. An insect is crawling out from under the rock and making its way across the ground to a particle of food. From your vantage point, you witness these events simultaneously. The rock, the insect, and the crumb are one event in your present experience. But for that insect, the rock is its past, the ground it's crawling over is its present, and the crumb is its future. If the insect could step off, or above, the path it is on, it too could switch off looking only at the one segment of life between its past and future; it could change its view to seeing it all simultaneously.

This simultaneous experiencing of time and perspective can happen to us in meditation or in moments of great joy and ecstasy. Past, present, and future merge into the eternal now. However, we often find that life has clouded our vision; we've lost the ability to step aside and look back and forth. We've even agreed to the mass hallucination that we can look in only one direction. We've made this decision in an ultimate act of free will that has had dangerous consequences.

If we are to believe our present science, there is nothing else like us in the universe. For sure there is nothing approaching us in our own world, and certainly on our own planet, earth. What separates us from everything else?

Free will.

We are the only species on the planet with the ability to make great life choices. Right or wrong, good or bad, these decisions are in our own hands. Think about it: A plant can't even choose to not absorb water that is poured on its roots. An animal that feels hunger and sees food cannot choose not to eat; if an animal is attacked, it cannot choose not to defend itself. The absorption of water, eating, self-defense, and other natural acts are in the nature of the species. They are in our nature as well. But our advanced program allows us to choose to starve ourselves or hurt ourselves or believe lies about ourselves.

Why do we ever choose what does not serve us?

I believe there are very good reasons, the most important being: That is how we grow.

George C. Wolfe once said, "The only thing you learn from being fabulous is how to be more fabulous. But hit an obstacle and you discover a stronger, better version of yourself." I believe that's what we are all here to do. And we do it by exercising our free will.

Say you've broken up with a cold, selfish, unloving partner and you don't want another one like that. Who do you think the next person you meet will be?

Another cold, selfish, unloving person.

Why?

Because

$$\text{New Intention} \rightarrow \text{Old Circumstance} < \begin{matrix} \text{Choose Different} \\ \text{Choose Same} \end{matrix}$$

When you set out with a new intention to change something in your life, your life as you've been living it shows up. But, because of your new intention, you now see it as the very thing you do not want. Before this moment you accepted it, and might have even enjoyed it or rationalized why it was that way. Only now it's staring you in the face in all its ugliness.

Has that ever happened to you?

But what did you expect? Did you really think all you had to do was think one new thought and—*bam!*—everything would instantly be different? Your life is constructed by decades of thoughts, day in and day out, hour by hour. Each thought was a direct mail-order request for exactly what you now have. Now you want to change subscriptions before the old ones have run out?

So the life you've been living, in the form of an old circumstance, shows right up. And here is the most critical moment of your life, the fork in the road. Here is where you make the decision, on a daily basis, to either live the life you've been living or to step into the frontier of the life of your dreams. What do you do?

Actually, most of us just renew our old subscriptions. We choose the same thing we've always had. It's what we've always known, even if we don't like it; it's what we're most comfortable with. "It hasn't been so bad, there's actually a lot of good in it," we tell ourselves. But really, we choose the same life we had already because of fear.

Keep doing what you've always done and you'll keep getting what you've always gotten. When you choose the same thing you've always had before, you exercise your free will in a way that sets you no higher than anything in the plant or animal kingdom.

But why, you cry, when you've tried to summon your true beloved, does another cold, selfish, unloving person have to appear? Because this presents you with a gift; it presents you with opportunity; this is the only way you get to be different from every other entity on the planet. Another cold, selfish, unloving person comes along so that you can exercise the right to do what you alone, as a human being, have the ability to do. He or she has come so that you can exercise your free will and choose something else.

Choose differently.

How do you demonstrate that you no longer want to be taken advantage of at work?

The next time someone at work asks you to do something that makes you feel put upon, you . . .

Choose differently.

How do you demonstrate that you want success and power and love and joy in your life right now?

The next time a "wonderful opportunity" comes along that will leave you emotionally drained, financially bereft, and no higher on your career ladder . . .

Choose differently.

The next time anything comes along that isn't success, power, love, joy, you need to exercise your free will to choose some other alternative.

The Psalms say, Think of the lilies of the field. They neither toil nor strain, yet nothing in the kingdom is more beautifully arrayed than these.

The lilies don't get to choose. They are beautiful. They can't choose to wilt today and bloom tomorrow, or maybe to turn out a dull gray. They are perfect in every way, every day.

The lilies remind me of the givingness of the universe. They remind me that only good is being prepared for each of us in every moment. It reminds me that I can have this—if I will choose it.

The lily doesn't have a choice, so it is perfect and beautiful all the time.

The price of our ability to choose is that sometimes we don't choose the good that has been prepared for us. It's still there waiting, waiting for us to turn around and receive it, waiting for us to choose differently. The fork in the road doesn't close because we walked off down the other path. We don't even have to go back. Another fork will appear.

No matter how many choices you make, the path to your good is always there waiting for you to choose it.

Will you choose it?

Or will you continue to hang on to stories and relationships and jobs and problems that you have also chosen to have?

Are you ready to choose joy? Are you ready to choose love?

Then let's rewrite history. Let's write your story as it would be if you knew you were as good as you are, because this is the truth. This is what is real. And nothing that is real can be destroyed. The truth does not change because you chose, some time in the past, not to believe in it.

I showed up at my spiritual center, *Agape,* in Los Angeles, one Sunday and found that every seat was covered with an envelope labeled "VIP RE-SERVED." There seemed to be nowhere for my friend and me to sit. We turned to an usher, looking quizzical, I'm sure. "Sit anywhere," he said as his arm displayed the whole expanse to us. "You are all the VIPs these seats are reserved for." Everyone inside the church was a VIP that day.

I sat down and hurriedly opened my envelope. Inside was an invitation to T. Harv Eker's seminar "Millionaire Mind Intensive." Not only was the offer free, but I could bring a friend. The friend sitting beside me had two envelopes on his seat. Although he was in severe financial trouble at that time, he sat inert even as I tried to share my excitement about attending the program. He didn't even open the envelope. "You can have these," he said, handing me the two unopened envelopes.

Now I had never heard of T. Harv Eker. I simply had a gut instinct that an opportunity to learn the principles of creating wealth—that happened to be occurring on my birthday—was a sign that the universe was talking to me. And I was sure going to pay attention.

So here I was with the ability to take five friends with me to a weekend workshop that promised to train us to become millionaires! Overjoyed, I quickly called a dear friend, Donna, in North Carolina. She and her partner, Bill, decided to fly to California with their teenage daughter, Carrie. I invited another friend, Joan, whose daughter went to school with my own. I also invited a friend whom I had worked with named Theresa.

Now, even though the workshop was free, there were still considerable obstacles to my attending. The biggest problem was that my first good job that year fell on the same weekend as the workshop, which also happened to be the weekend of my fortieth birthday.

But to me, the birthday was a divine sign that I was destined to be at the workshop. So, even though I would lose a week of work, I reasoned that the lost week's work would be nothing compared to the wealth I would accumulate after taking this course. The second obstacle was that I couldn't afford lodging; my friends and I would have to drive four hours round-trip while attending a twelve-hour daily workshop, and we'd have to maintain that schedule for three days. But nothing was going to stand in my way.

Joan drove her own car. Donna, Bill, Carrie, and I car-pooled and brought bag lunches. Theresa lived about fifteen minutes from the workshop location, so she wouldn't face these same problems, luckily.

When I arrived at the hotel for registration early on the first day, I was extraordinarily impressed by the organization of the facilitators. There were some two thousand people there, and they registered us all and had name tags ready. Donna and Bill didn't have their e-mail confirmations, but they swiftly registered them anyway.

The one person I didn't see was Theresa. I couldn't imagine why she wasn't there, but as the meeting was beginning, I asked if I could pick up her registration so that if she came in a bit late, she could walk right in. They agreed, and I went in expecting to see her any moment. So in I went holding my registration as well as Theresa's, and for the first hour I kept an eye out for her.

I never saw her.

After that first day, I was so blown away by the material being taught that, as late as it was when I got home, I e-mailed Theresa to ask where she had been.

The e-mail I got back from her said that she had never received a confirmation of her registration. She said, "I thought about just driving by, but I didn't. I figured if I wasn't registered, I wouldn't get in."

I was astounded. I asked Theresa why she thought she was blocking herself from this opportunity to learn skills that she said she truly desired and desperately needed. In return, she got very huffy with me and shot back: "They e-mailed me that you never registered me and I even called and no one called me back. I'm not blocking anything!" Later she forwarded me the e-mails, giving me the evidence, so to speak. But all I could think was that Donna and Bill had flown across the country without e-mail confirmations because they were determined to get the benefits that were being offered. Here she was, fifteen minutes away. Wasn't the opportunity to learn to think like a millionaire worth a fifteen- or thirty-minute drive? I never said any of this to her.

I thought it was over until another week went by and Theresa forwarded me an e-mail from the company telling her that she was definitely never registered, and giving her the names of the people I had registered, which of course did not include her.

I figured this was her way of proving that she hadn't been blocking anything. The "reality" was: NO REGISTRATION for her. Therefore she had been "right" to not bother to drive over to the hotel.

Let me go off on a brief tangent. Quantum physicists have demonstrated that a single particle can be in two places at exactly the same time. In fact, they can photograph it. Impossible, you say.

Theresa was my demonstration of two simultaneous realities coexisting. Theresa was in one reality—not registered to attend the workshop and therefore correct for not showing up (with the e-mail to prove it)—yet in another reality, the registration was in my hand, and I was in that workshop waiting for her. Had Theresa chosen to show up despite the lack of registration or confirmation, in this alternate reality, where I was waiting for her, the registration was waiting for her, too.

Theresa chose to be right rather than to be rich.

What do you choose?

Did you know there is a very good reason why we choose that which does not serve us? Psychologists have a term for it: "secondary gains."

You see, you might not have the man or woman of your dreams, but in place of that, you may have lots of empathy. That can come in the form of compliments from friends telling you what a great catch you are; anybody would be lucky to have you. Or maybe it comes in the form of the sympathy you get for all the bad men or women you've been with. You have people telling you how undeserving and unappreciative those misfits were. These kinds of gifts, strangely enough, have enormous power over our lives. They may actually keep us stuck in old patterns and stories that block our good.

When I was letting go of the story of being the victim of my former partner, I realized that my "secondary gains" were that many people admired and were inspired by my warrior mystique and my stoic ability to take on the legal system. My father told me that I was the strongest person he knew. He said, "Most people who have gone through what you have gone through would have killed themselves, killed someone else, or become drug addicts." I felt so proud of that! It was the kindest thing he had ever said to me. And he said it right before he died. So of course I wanted to live up to the compliment.

But, living up to it meant I had to keep being strong in the face of obstacles that would have turned most people into suicidal murderers or drug addicts. And that was the life I created for myself for several years: filled with obstacles to overcome, besieged but admirable, brave, steadfast, tormented, and inspirational. I wanted to live up to my father's accolade; I wanted to believe I was everything my father had said I was.

Now how sane is that?

But aren't you doing that somewhere in your life?

Paying everybody else's bills while you can't get ahead because you're such a "saint"?

Caring for the "helpless" and ungrateful because you're the most generous person anybody knows?

Solving everybody else's problems while your doctor bills are soaring for migraines and ulcers?

I had to decide that I didn't want, or need, my hallmark to be "strong or inspiring." I had to give up the "admire and inspire" label. I had to discover that I didn't really want to be admired for all the hardships I'd endured. That wasn't the mark I wanted to leave.

I remember the moment when the shift was complete.

It took years for that moment to arrive. I would take one step forward, two steps back. It's how we grow, if we keep practicing the processes. But that moment did come.

One night after my Broadway performance, I had a driver who was rude and cantankerous the whole drive home. He kept arguing with me: He was sure I didn't live where I said I lived; he took me well out of my way and wasn't sorry. After that, I told the car service to never send me that driver again. Whenever I needed a driver, the dispatcher would say, "It says not to send car 461; why, what happened?" I refused to donate any energy to the matter by discussing it.

Then another night, at midnight, after a grueling twelve-hour day, all I wanted to do was to get home so I could wake up at six and start all over again. Yet who should be waiting for me but car number 461? By the time I found out he was there, he had already pissed off the doorman and several others at the theater. The doorman had called the company and requested another car, but they said I would have to wait another hour.

This was my fork in the road. I was tired. I was stressed out. I wanted to go home. If I waited another hour, it would be two hours before I got home, at 2:00 a.m. The unacceptable driver was staring at me. The "good girl" in me thought it was awfully rude to just refuse to ride with him. But then I heard myself writing the story I would tell everyone about my miserable ride home, and I caught myself.

I could choose the old circumstance, being victimized and surviving it and telling a great story to make everyone laugh or commiserate; or I could choose differently. Of course, choosing differently meant waiting longer to get home. But more important, it meant choosing my happiness and comfort over placating someone who had been very unkind to me. So I told the service to send another car, and actually it arrived in forty-five minutes.

Feelings: Choosing differently meant expecting the car company to pay for their error. Choosing differently meant not needing to make everyone groan or laugh at another story of my misfortune, because I was no longer choosing misfortune.

Are you ready to do that?

Are you ready to turn down misfortune, even when it's easier to accept than waiting for your good?

A part of me died that night—a part that was no longer serving me. We'll talk about that in the next chapter. What died was the part that needed to be polite, to grin and bear it so everyone could compliment me on how "easy" I was. 'Cause it's often easier to be a victim.

Let others do as they please with you, and they'll "love" you for it. And it goes deeper than this. How many times have you said "yes" to something you didn't really agree with or want to do, because it was easier than saying "no"? Because no one would require an explanation. And saying "no" might invite someone's ire. You could do it; it's not that hard, right? Until they ask the third, fourth, fifth time, and then comes the time when you drop the nuclear bomb on them with a hysterical NO! NO NO NO!!

Then they look at you like you're crazy.

And you know what: You are. See, they're just doing what they've always been doing, no more, no less. Now you're the one who's out of control.

Why?

Because you kept exercising your free will to choose the same path, over and over, a path you never wanted and didn't like the first time, and it got geometrically worse each time after that, and now it's *their fault*.

But you chose it.

Sonya went to a massage parlor. She felt she was generous for tipping 20 percent, but the proprietor suggested she give 25 percent. The first time this happened, she felt offended and refused. By the next visit, however, she had justified to herself the idea of the larger gratuity: After all, the women who worked there were low-paid and the massage price was also low, justifying the larger tip. When she went for her next massage, she felt proud and generous for giving the previously requested 25 percent tip.

This time, however, the masseuse herself requested a 30 percent tip. Sonya refused, and as she left, the tension quickly reentered her body as she engaged in angry arguments with herself about the audacity of the masseuse, the experience, the reaction, the quandary: Should she perhaps call the Better Business Bureau?

Sonya and I had been working on her ability to access her authentic desires and to respond from what she wanted, rather than to repeatedly *react* to external circumstances. She told me, "All of a sudden it hit me. The masseuse was just asking me for what she wanted. It wasn't personal. And why shouldn't she be able to ask for what she wanted? I was the one who had the problem: saying no. So I didn't know how to act. I couldn't respond from my own position—a tip is a gift and not a requirement, so I can give what I feel comfortable with—so her request threw me. I felt pressured and angry with her for even asking for more than I wanted to give, because in my world, it's an unreasonable request. Suddenly my memory flashed back to a dozen other times when I got angry because someone asked for what they wanted, because I couldn't do that for myself. I also saw a number of situations that had upset me a lot, and realized they were not personal, either. I knew this was my work: to learn to respond from what I wanted, independent of what others want, independent of others' possible reactions to what I want."

What a revelation Sonya had as she strode away from that massage parlor in the midst of her disturbed internal monologue. People have the right to ask for what they want. If you give it to them, they assume you're okay with it, and they probably will ask again. Wouldn't you?

So why do we give things when we're not okay with it?

Because of the secondary gains or because somewhere, sometime, it got us what we wanted or kept us from something we definitely didn't want. The button is hard-wired. It's part of the autonomic system now. You've been a doormat so many times that when the doorbell buzzes, you just lie down.

Until one day you don't lie down, and then everybody has hell to pay.

Do you see how we do this to ourselves?

Do you see how we choose our own poison? And blame somebody else for administering it?

CHOOSE DIFFERENTLY.

One of the most powerful ways we can exercise our free will is by choosing to complete all our communications, past, present, or future. Every button that triggers us is the result of an incomplete communication.

It's an incomplete communication when you do something you don't want to do, but choose to do because of genuine kindness or generosity. If you could share your genuine desire *not* to do something, often people will be understanding.

This is hard to do, I know, because the hard-wired button triggers automatically. Yet the person who asked you to volunteer for her child's class party/join his reading and discussion group/help her niece find a summer job may not even want you to go against your truth. Once you say you can't do it, their response may be different; your choices are different; everything's different.

Barbara had run the annual block club flea market every year since it began, and the truth was that she never enjoyed it. She originally took it on because a conflict had arisen that threatened the whole event, and she stepped in to restore order. But then she got saddled with it over and over again. Years passed, everyone assumed the flea market was her baby, and she no longer believed she had a choice about it. In her steadfast, stoic way, she collected everybody's junk, sorted it, priced it, labeled it, and sold it, and then was responsible for disposing of the useless leftovers at the end. She said, "At the end of the party, I didn't want to see or speak to my neighbors for another year."

Barbara had been hard-wired to please people. Her older brother and sister were both disappointments to her parents, so she had been their "good"—albeit miserable—girl. I asked her what would happen if she simply shared her feelings about how hard it was to do the flea market and asked for some help. "No, no. Nobody wants to do this crap; that's why I'm stuck with it. It brings in the most money for the community, and if I didn't do it, the whole event would probably get scrapped."

I urged her to speak with her neighbors about her aversion and see what happened. It was a terrifying moment for her. She could not recall a single instance in her life when she described feeling negative about a chore required of her by others. She had always stifled her objections and responded willingly to others' needs. But she got up her courage and spoke to the block club.

It turned out that many people didn't really like the way she ran the flea market. They thought it could be done better, and believed they knew how to make it earn more. They hadn't mentioned any of this to Barbara, though, for fear of hurting her feelings by taking it away from her! She said, "At first I was pissed; then I was hurt; but then I got excited about all the new ideas they had for making it run better and make more money."

Barbara still works on the flea market, but now she has help and she doesn't hate it anymore. What about you?

Isn't that a novel idea? Here you've been doing something you don't like just to make someone happy (and then they're very happy and perhaps even grateful to you, though I'm sure you don't get much pleasure out of that appreciation). But now you share your discomfort and they may apologize for having asked; they may even say they don't want you to do the favor because they are genuinely concerned with your comfort.

It's scary to risk, of course, because it might turn out much worse than that, as you feared. The person may respond with anger and harsh words. But when you choose the same way of doing things as you have always chosen before, you know exactly how it's going to turn out: with your feeling angry and put-upon and blaming them for it.

The world of your being put-upon and the world of your being valued exist simultaneously, waiting for you to choose between them.

Caleb drifted from job to job, never staying with anything longer than six months. He told me he had wanted to be an engineer but he hadn't been accepted at any of the colleges he applied to, so he got a job around his neighborhood and lived at home taking care of his mother.

Caleb didn't have much energy. He wasn't very passionate about anything. But there was a flicker when he talked about the things he had once dreamed of building. I asked why he hadn't built them anyway. He had the usual excuses, but in particular, he was sure that no one would give him a chance to do anything without an engineering degree. His rejection letters from several schools were, for him, irrefutable evidence that he could never get a degree. So he just crawled through life, never trying to do much of anything, constantly fearing failure.

Caleb came to see me shortly after his mother died. He was in the throes of a violent rage, alternately screaming and nearly breaking down in tears. His speech was incomprehensible. Finally, when he calmed down enough to make himself understood, he explained. In the process of cleaning out his mother's things, he found a box with his name on it. Inside were awards he never knew he had received, and at the very bottom were acceptance letters to every university he had applied to. His grief over his mother's death and his grief over her betrayal left him inconsolable. How could he forgive her? How could he ever be complete with her? How could he go on with such a failed life?

Many people walk around in a world of imagined insecurity and even misery. Many of our most important communications are incomplete; that's what grief and guilt are made of. When things don't turn out the way we would have liked them to, we suffer.

Sometimes we try to complete our communication with another person and things only get worse; the miscommunication is exacerbated. The beauty of this next process is that it works for you, and does not even require the participation of the other person involved in the original distress-producing incident.

How is that possible?

The pain you feel is centered inside your brain. Doctor Joseph Dispenza has told us that the brain doesn't know the difference between a "real" experience and the experience represented by our memory of the event.

Now memory, we all can agree, can be colored so that it can almost be like imagination. The brain cannot always distinguish between the two. Thus Caleb lived his life imagining, really, that he was not good enough to become an engineer. But after twenty years of living as an inadequate person in the disdainful world, Caleb now had a chance to choose a brave new world, one that would support his desire to live his life to the fullest. Indeed he did. He reapplied to engineering school and began to brush up on his high school course work. He chose freedom over fear, dharma over drama. You can too.

"Oh," you say, "but I've tried talking to [whoever it is] and no way am I doing that again." You don't have to. Because you're right: If it's not going to work, you can't make it work. You could try to tell someone you forgive him, and accidentally start a huge conflict because he may not perceive having done anything to be forgiven for. You could set yourself up for another injury!

So how do you complete a communication if not with the other person? You do it yourself. After all, the incompleteness is in your mind. It is not "over there" with the other person. You can reach completion in your own mind.

When I chose not to need to be admired for my strength at fighting the system and overcoming hardship, I completed communications with many people who would never have taken part in the healing process with me. The judge who awarded custody to my sons' father would not have finally given me a chance to be heard; his mind was made up against me. The process had to be mine; the shift happened in my mind. It didn't matter what anyone else would think about what I did when I changed worlds. I didn't have to tell anyone who was victimizing me, "Hey, I know I did this to myself. Sorry for blaming you." The work I did was within myself and for myself, and the process in this chapter is part of it.

For years, I had walked around bad-mouthing the government and the law. Then I did the work—the internal work, the private work—to let that story go. I couldn't right wrongs or change the court system, but I could right myself and change my life.

What happened? Within weeks, governmental benevolence appeared to me as if by magic. The government hadn't changed. *I* had changed. Those programs that helped people were there all along, but as long as I was choosing victimization to overcome and be admired for, I couldn't receive the good that was waiting for me.

Choose differently.

So how do these buttons get installed to run/ruin our lives?

More important: How do we de-install them?

Gregory's mother left him to live with his grandmother when he was a small boy. He missed her desperately and longed for her all his life; every girlfriend he had seemed to be a repeat of his mother: another treasured woman who would abandon him. When Gregory finally married a woman he adored, she left him, ostensibly because she didn't want children, but then she had a child with another man. Gregory wore his wedding ring for years after the divorce and kept his wedding certificate in full view, enshrined on the mantle. Wonderful women came into his life, but he could not stay interested in them because he wanted the one who didn't want him. He was still trying recapture the love of the mother who had left him.

When we are caught in the pain of the past, it is as if it plays over and over again. Hopelessly we keep doing what we tried in the past. Even if it never worked before, we expect it to work now. Of course it doesn't work now either, but we can't stop ourselves.

Have you done this?

Have you asked for support from someone who has never given it in the past and has no likelihood of doing it now?

Have you ever shared your joy with someone who has never showed happiness over your success?

It's the same as an addictive/allergic response. We crave or compulsively use the substance that hurts us because some part of us believes that if we just do it enough, we will desensitize ourselves out of the negative reaction. It doesn't work.

You are unconsciously trying to desensitize yourself in order to reach completion. But because the event of the past is over, and you don't recognize its shadow in the scene before you, you cannot find completion for it in this new set of circumstances. And while you keep trying an old way in a new world, you unconsciously botch this situation, which then reinforces the old button and creates a new button around an entirely new set of circumstances.

But you are free to choose to do it differently at any time.

Are you ready to choose differently right now?

We've all gone into jobs and relationships, letting the other folks know what happened "the last time"—as if that is their warning about what we won't accept this time. Fifty percent of all marriages end in divorce. If that statistic means anything, it means this: Despite our "warnings," at least half of us keep choosing the same relationship that reflects a prior unsuccessful relationship. As long as we live in fear that this moment can turn out like our troubled "last time," we are robbed of the experience of the now. Instead, we spend our lives in the broken record of pain, disappointment, and betrayal, trying to fix in the now what we could not fix back then.

Are you ready to break that cycle so that you can respond to what you want, rather than react to what other people want?

Well, the benevolence of the universe is such that if you don't get it right the first time, you'll probably have plenty of other opportunities to try it, again and again, until you prevail.

Shortly after my divorce and custody battle, I began dating a new man. Seemingly as different from my ex as anyone could be, this man had witnessed my pain and sorrow over the loss of my first two children, and had even tried to help me at times. We eventually had a child together. When our marriage ended, though, what do you think he said?

"I want custody of our daughter."

My old pattern would have been rage, hysteria, even more intense fighting than before, because I had a recent experience of how badly it could turn out if I lost control over my contact with my child. Furthermore, this man was a shrewd businessman, trained in the ways of winning.

But I had done the mental work that I am about to share with you, and because of this process, the trouble-button that was with me since the early childhood absence of my own father, and the trouble-button of terror at becoming a "crazy single mother," and even the newly wired trouble-button of losing my children, were disconnected, and could not control my choices or my behavior anymore.

The demand for my child occurred over the phone. I knew, suddenly, that I was entering unknown territory. At first, I wasn't sure I heard him right, and so I said, "Excuse me?" Firmly, with careful enunciation and even more careful emphasis, he made clear what he wanted.

"I am taking custody of our daughter. I will be filing papers this week, and my lawyer will contact yours."

Suddenly I knew exactly which fork in the road to take. I delivered my response in the sweetest and softest of voices: "Oh you don't need to do that, because I'm never setting foot in a court again. Just come and get her."

Silence.

"Come and get her."

His next words lacked the bravado and assurance of the prior declaration: "You can't just walk away from your baby!"

"Sure I can; people do it every day. Come get her."

Silence.

I continued in a businesslike tone: "I'll have her bags packed. Let me know when I can see her."

"Well, you can see her whenever you want."

"Oh no, you're the boss now. You just write it up and let me know when."

Silence.

"Pick her up. I'll get her bags packed."

"Now, now Tonya, I'm not trying to keep you away from your daughter, I . . ."

"Pick her up."

Silence.

He truly did not know what to say. It was aikido, where you defeat your opponent by moving with their force, rather than against it.

He picked up our baby and kept her for about two weeks. When he brought her back, I unpacked her bags and kept living my life as her mother. I have never had another instance like that again.

What happened? I chose differently. My old pattern had been

Feel → react → think (later).

My new healthy pattern is

Feel → think → act.

The old buttons that had been there for anyone to push—the old buttons that would send me into automatic tailspins so that others could predict my behavior more than I could choose my behavior—had all been disconnected. I was a free woman: Even though circumstances could still be negative, I didn't have to react and make the choices that created more negatives. I could even make a terrible situation into a positive experience.

Armed with the faith that comes from positive experience, when I next went to court with my other children's father, I was ready.

The hearing was bizarre and, like many court proceedings, horrible. My ex had decided, after many years of allowing visitation, that I shouldn't see my children at all; he refused to turn them over for visits. When I tried to get into court, I faced months of waiting and many postponements. Finally I stood before the judge, who did not want to hear any evidence or make any tough decisions. My ex wanted me to have only supervised visitation, in a room with a DCFS officer, for an hour or so now and then, but he had no legal basis for that demand, not having any evidence of unfitness. To make me cave in, he had kept the children away from me for nearly a year, dangling "supervised visitation" like a prize.

The judge tried to intimidate me into accepting his terms: "Ms. Pinkins, you have not seen your children for so long, and the father is willing to give you supervised visits. Why not take it? You can have a supervised visit right now; I can set it up in ten minutes. Why don't you take it?"

It was a very difficult moment; I was desperate to see my children. But my past desperate reactions had only made my problems worse. The judge was not ordering me into supervised visitation, she was asking me to choose it. She had the power to order it, but she wanted me to choose it.

Life is always giving us the chance to exercise our free will. Now in this situation, I had fought for a year to get access to my children, and an appeals court order said I was entitled to normal unsupervised visitation, but what is a court order? It's a piece of paper that you have to go back to court to get another piece of paper to enforce, if the adversary will not willingly comply. Realistically, my choice was either supervised visits if and when my ex allows them, or more time spent in court, trying to get what the last court had already ordered.

So I had to choose. I felt sad, angry, frustrated. In the past I would have reacted first and thought about the consequences afterward. But now I was feeling, then thinking, so I could choose how to act. Should I go against the very thing I desired and believed I deserved: the right to see my children freely? Should I choose to comply with demands and requirements that should never have been placed on me? Should I, an African-American mother, agree to visit my children in a locked room with an armed guard, showing them that I—we—were not free to have our relationship on our own terms? Or should I choose to refuse these "options" and really make a choice? Should I hold out in faith that I would receive what I desired and what I knew I absolutely deserved?

My dilemma was great. When I was standing in line an hour earlier, to go through the metal detector and into the courthouse, my children walked by. The younger one broke loose from his father's hand and ran into my embrace, burying his face in my neck wordlessly, holding me in a grip nothing could have shaken. My arms were around him and we were breathing each other in through our heavy winter clothing as if we had never been torn apart. Standing before the judge, I could still feel the pressure of his cheek and the moisture from his eyelids. I could still see in my mind's eye my older boy as he gazed longingly at me from several yards away, but hesitated to follow his little brother. The judge was about as far from me as my older boy had been at that moment.

This, or that? One choice or another? What feels so good that it is practically impossible to turn from it, or what is so frightening that it is nearly impossible to contemplate? The immediate gratification of having my children in my arms again, in spite of the locked door and armed guard, or the terrible risk: saying no, and then being ordered into supervised visitation anyway or, even worse, another week, month, year, decade without contact with my boys. The excruciating moment drew itself out into an excruciating minute.

Before I go on, let me point something out: Because I had done the mental work that I'm about to take you through, I felt no fear that I could not live with whatever choice I made. I knew in that moment-turned-to-minute that I would make a choice and I would survive it, as would my children. Therefore I still had free will, which could not be taken from me. See, there was no button for my adversaries to push. They could set up the circumstances, they could make a bad situation, but I did not have to react as they had designed, and I did not have to make the situation worse. I was not reacting, but responding, proactively, to achieve what I wanted, rather than giving in to the fear that had dominated me in the past. No longer did I believe that I had better take "something—anything!" rather than risk ending up with the very thing I did not want.

How many times have you been in that situation? Not wanting what is offered, but afraid that it's as good as it will ever get? That fear is fraught with emotion, and it can block your thinking completely. You are so sure that no other option is possible that you in fact react against your own best interests.

We'll talk a lot about fear in a later chapter, but for now, suffice it to say that the universe does not communicate through anxiety. If you're afraid when there's no immediate danger, it's not a message from the universe that you're hearing.

Gavin de Becker, one of the nation's top criminal profilers, wrote in his book *The Gift of Fear* that what most of us call fear is really anxiety and worry, emotions that serve no good purpose. Genuine fear, which, as he describes it, is more of an instinctual response so rapid and automatic that it lacks reason, is still necessary for survival. But he points out that this real form of fear has been almost socialized out of our beings. So much so that de Becker says he can usually discover who is stalking someone in the very first interview with the victim. Amazing?

De Becker says that genuine fear is gut instinct, not usually connected to any logical, rational circumstance in the moment. Therefore, most of us ignore it. An expert at finding information that hides unaware inside a person, de Becker might ask a crime victim, "Is there anyone you thought it could be?" She might answer, "I thought about so and so, but . . . no, he would never . . ." Nearly 100 percent of the time, that person who "would never . . ." is the one!

So if most of our appropriate fear responses have been suppressed by conditioning, what is that feeling that grabs us, fills us with emotion, drives us to do things we think are necessary because we somehow muster up a reason and rationale to convince ourselves they're in our best interests—when they're not? If we are being spun around and tossed like Ping-Pong balls by the events around us, if we cannot make our own decisions about what is best to do, we lose our ability to respond well to opportunities that are always surrounding us. Healthy people respond to circumstances; dysfunctional people only react.

I love this phrase from Al-Anon: "If it's hysterical, it's historical." When you do not complete a communication on the spot, it becomes magnified, so the next time a similar situation occurs you may overreact and have a "global response." According to Dr. Pat Allen, psychotherapist and relationship expert, you may hear yourself say, "you always" or "you never."

If it's hysterical, it's historical. Anything that sets you off your rocker in a given moment is connected to a moment from your past. There are the hot zones, the buttons that say: "The terrible thing is happening again. Stop it, nuke it now!"

Your father told you, "Speak that way in my house, and it's the highway for you." Now, when your children "speak that way," you are immediately triggered into the anxiety you experienced in the past. Unconsciously you act as if you are right, because you're sure you are, since in your past your very survival depended on your behaving in the appropriate way. Never mind the fact that "speaking that way" might have referred only to childish use of "potty" words or naming body parts or calling something a "lie." Your life depended on not doing it, so when your own children do it today, that same fight-or-flight syndrome kicks in.

If you are fraught with emotion over a decision in the present moment, consider this possibility: *Maybe it has nothing to do with the present moment. Perhaps you are reacting to a perceived consequence based on your memory of a historical event.* Or maybe your reaction to your present environment comes from a leftover habit, or even from a desire to reverse it.

If you keep your attention in the present situation, and you respond in the here and now, while really listening to, and paying attention to, your feelings and perceptions, you can actually "know" more than you know. When you were a teenager, your parents probably worried about you more than you would like: Don't do this, don't do that, don't walk alone, particularly in the dark. Committed to writing and running your own programs instead of those installed by others, you have practiced doing exactly what you've been taught not to do.

Say you were walking home late at night and you approached a block without streetlights. But you're not afraid of dark streets because since you were on your own, you have tested that and found that not every dark street is dangerous. Now suppose you approached that same street one night, but before turning the corner, you had a sudden impulse to drop in on a friend who lives across town, or you ran back to pick up an item you forgot. If, later, you learned that something untoward had actually happened on that block that night, you would have experienced the universe talking to you: by sending you a positive impulse that protected you from a negative situation. This is fear in its proper place, filling its proper function. The universe is always sending you messages to go in the right direction, to avoid many dangers, to fulfill your highest and best desires, and to keep yourself well and safe. But it's up to you at every point to choose to follow those directions. Here's one of my favorite acronyms:

Face
Everything
And
Recover

If we truly faced every experience before us, we would recover from each and every one. And if "recovery" calls to your mind a healing from a serious injury, try replacing that idea with the "recovery" that happens in sports when one team is in the lead but the winds suddenly turn.

Back to the courtroom: The judge is screaming at the top of her lungs and turning beet red. (Yes, judges do that, and she had a particular reputation for tantrums on the bench.) She's telling me that she's not making any new orders because I have visitation already, and I can have a supervised visit right now.

I had to choose between a supervised visit with my babies or saying no and walking out of court not knowing when I would see them again.

I know what most people would do. I did not. I stood up in the court and said, "I have court orders for visitation, but they are not being obeyed. You have the power to enforce them, and you will not. Well, I am not going to have my children see their mother in a room under lock and key as if she were a criminal. That might make them think they were criminals themselves. So if you refuse to enforce my court-ordered rights, I guess I won't see my children until they are old enough to walk into a room and visit me themselves."

Everyone was outraged. The judge, lawyers, and law guardians began begging me to take just this one supervised visit. I had to choose between what was my right and what I would accept, or taking whatever they would dish out.

Here was my fork in the road. I had to choose: Choose the Same, or Choose Different?

At first glance, it might appear that accepting supervised visitation was actually choosing differently, for I had refused it for a year.

But choosing differently is not about a change in action, it is about a change in the *pattern of being*. My pattern had been to be a victim. To accept supervised visitation would have been volunteering, with my own free will, to continue that pattern of victimization. Cognitive therapy is based on the idea that, no matter how bad you're feeling, changing your behavior will alter your thoughts and feelings. In fact, what you do alters your brain chemistry, which in turn gives you a different take on your circumstances.

My different choice was refusing to be a victim, and demanding, instead, what I had already won, and refusing to accept anything less. This was no easy decision with a five- and a seven-year-old staring at me, weeping. But the choices for exponential growth and power are rarely easy.

The universe is benevolent about giving you only as big a problem as you can deal with.

The good news is that as you successfully manage bigger problems, you invite bigger successes, greater wealth, and more opportunity.

How could I choose not to see my children under "any circumstances"? Remember the movie *Sophie's Choice*? In the face of terrible circumstances, Sophie had exercised her power to choose which of her children would live, which would perish. Doing so destroyed her own life.

How does this relate?

Choice must always be for the highest and greatest good of the self, or it is no choice.

Viktor Frankl, in *Man's Search for Meaning*, talks about the daily choices concentration camp prisoners had to make in order to survive. He said that when they saw a man lying in bed smoking a cigarette, they knew he had made a choice to die. Who are we to say whether the choice to die in those circumstances is not the better choice? But Frankl posits that we not ask the question what we should expect out of life. Life expects each one of us to fulfill a unique purpose, and if we choose not to fulfill it, it never gets done.

We fulfill it by our choices. Every act of free will moves us ahead on the path of our evolution.

CHOOSE DIFFERENTLY.

Prisoners of war are often given choices between mutually negative consequences. Why? Because the captor knows that whatever amount of free will the prisoner is allowed to exercise strengthens him and keeps him around to be used for the captor's own ends. In these situations, of course, the choice is not an act of free will.

Sophie did not act out of free will; she had none. When you or I repeat our actions from a previous time in our own history, we are not acting out of free will: We are captives in our own tragedies, where we play both captor and victim.

True free will includes the choice to refuse to choose. That's what separates us from the rest of the plant and animal kingdom. We can choose, or refuse to choose; even that is a choice.

For Sophie, whose own life was at stake, choosing between her son and her daughter gave her a false sense of power and control over her life. She chose the possible secondary gain of finding favor with the guard and perhaps saving her son.

How can we not be like Sophie when we are both captor and guard? Sometimes choosing differently lies in refusing to choose, or in choosing the very thing that appears to be the worst choice.

For Sophie, refusing to choose might have meant saying, "You have power to take all our lives. I will not choose. Let that crime lie on your soul." Instead, by her "choice," she laid the crime on her own soul, and she destroyed her life by doing so.

For me, choosing differently when the judge had the power to order supervised visitation meant refusing to voluntarily accept it. For me, free choice meant refusing to take the false choices offered to me. Instead, I stated that even if I was ordered to take supervised visits, I would not obey; rather, I would wait to see my children free of bonds.

In what may appear to be an act of powerlessness may lie our greatest power: the power to harness and retrain our free will and use it for our own good. It is the road less traveled. It is the difference between the unexamined life and the good life.

How did my case turn out? The judge did not order me into supervised visitation. She ordered fifty-fifty visitation. My gamble paid off with increased time with my boys, from four days to fifteen days each month.

We all have the right to the best and brightest lives, though often we choose to accept far less. All of the incomplete communications of our lives installed buttons that anyone can push until we de-install them.

It's easier than you think.

This process, developed by John W. James and Russell Friedman, is used in their grief recovery books and programs. The process, mostly done alone without involving the other person at the end of the incomplete communication, allows you to de-install buttons and thereby get control over the pain, rage, fear, and anger that may control your life. The buttons that force you to automatically do what you've always been doing—and therefore to get what you've always been getting—are the buttons that take you out: out of joy, freedom, love, and prosperity.

There's a lot of good waiting to come your way. So you'd better get started.

Are you ready to choose differently?

This process takes place in four parts. First, choose a relationship that triggers you. You may not want to start with the all-out-war relationships, but if you're brave enough, go for it. In all probability these relationships were between you and your mother, father, step-parent, brother, sister, in-law, partner, former partner, child, grandparent, teacher, or best friend. (For me, it was my father.) This relationship will not be with your manicurist, gardener, babysitter, or any other nonessential person. That is, a person you can choose to keep in your life or not. We're talking about an essential relationship here, one that means a lot to you. So the relationship must be with someone who has had a significant impact on your life. You will have heard this person say things, seen them do things, and witnessed them modeling for you the way the world works in their eyes.

Let's stay on task for the big work: We're going to be performing psychic surgery, so don't get distracted by a corn on your toe. Corns are not deadly. The person was a great force in your life, and the incomplete communication occupies a great territory in your soul.

Have you chosen somebody?

Good.

The first step is to create a time line of your relationship with the person. The time line will go from the day you met up to the present moment. If you met at birth, start it there. If you met when you were ten years old, start it there. Whatever age you were when the person came into your life, that's where your time line begins.

Now the time line ends in the present moment, or whenever that person ceased to be a part of your life. If they died, what age were you when they died? That is when your time line ends. Note: Just because you don't see or speak with someone, does not mean they are out of your life. If you still hear about them, talk about them to other people, run into them on occasion, or even have some third-party contact, they are still a part of your life, so end your time line in the present.

Your time line is a horizontal line across the page.

Now you will begin making vertical lines above and below the horizontal line to coincide with remembered events in your relationship with your chosen person. The vertical marks above the horizontal line will represent POSITIVE events and the vertical lines below the horizontal line will represent NEGATIVE events.

All relationships contain both positive and negative events. Be sure to find both. If you need more paper, use more paper.

TIME LINE

FIRST   PRESENT
ENCOUNTER

The vertical marks you make should be as comprehensive as possible, representing remembered events, stories you do not personally remember but which were told to you, as well as imagined events of which you are uncertain.

The length of the vertical line will correspond to the positive or negative intensity of the event. If the event is very positive, the vertical mark extends high above the horizontal. If it's very negative, the mark falls far below the horizontal line. Many events will be rather neutral and the lines will be of short or medium length.

You are to continue adding events on the time line until you have charted the entire relationship. This could take a few minutes, a few hours, or even several days. Don't stop until you're sure you have been complete, but don't let it go on beyond a few days.

You will remember some of these events with the force of emotion you felt when you first experienced them. You will remember forgotten events, both positive and negative. Note every one of them and make its mark. We want the most accurate possible map of the relationship. We want to see where the buttons are, and when they were installed. Beside each vertical line you will write, in a few words, the event that coincides with it. Especially write down the ones you don't believe could have happened.

When you are done, you will have a life map of a relationship that caused great joy and great sorrow. More important, you will have a map of many of the buttons that take you out of the life you deserve to be living.

Maybe you're laughing at a wonderful thing you just remembered. Perhaps you're crying about a terrible thing you'd forgotten about, that just broke upon your consciousness and hurts again.

Are you still in the game?

Is this too messy? Too hard? Too painful? Too much work?

Then you have taken yourself out. So you can stop blaming THAT PERSON, whoever he or she is. If you can't look at your own self with depth and clarity, why should someone else want you to run their company, be their partner, or raise their children?

I've been saying that what you have gotten is what you have ordered, right? You can't necessarily choose whom you'll meet, but you can choose whom you'll choose. So you have made a time line's worth of choices and chosen experiences in your life. Are you curious about how the bill got filled?

I should have warned you that at this point, there is no turning back. Like that time you bought a red car to make sure you were driving something distinctive—and the next day you saw them everywhere. Just drive on; it will still get you where you need to go.

Now you are aware that you have buttons. And when they get pushed, from now on, even while you have the feelings that you habitually have while you react, or even while you overreact, you will be aware that there is another way. But, if you don't keep doing this big work, if you don't move along to de-install the buttons, you can avoid the work, but you can't avoid the triggers. So they will grow, and you won't get over them, and you won't get into control of your life, and the triggers will get bigger. That's my pep talk to keep you on task. Remember, it's surgery. If a surgeon opened you up and then figured the work was too hard and left the operating room with you still on that table, you'd be in some fix, wouldn't you? Don't do that to yourself.

Remember, the universe is doing everything it can to get you your good. If you run away from a four-hundred-pound gorilla, though, it will send you a two-ton elephant. And still, you will be able to handle it, because you were able to handle the gorilla but you forgot to—

Face
Everything
And
Recover.

That's what this fear of starting the process is made of, really. You doubt that it will work. You doubt that you can handle it. Let that serve you, too. Take the DOUBT and DOUBT IT.

DOUBT THE DOUBT.

Your fear says, "I can't do this."
Tell yourself "I doubt that."
Doubt the doubt.
So finish your time line. Cry, laugh, keep at it, go back to it, whatever it takes, but get it done.
Now that your time line is completed, congratulate yourself.
Take your right hand and pat yourself on the back. Now, put both hands together and give yourself a round of applause. *Right now.*
Do you feel good?
The hardest part is over. The rest is a piece of cake. Now that you have done the time line with one relationship, you can do it with every other one of the relationships that have left buttons that trigger you. You should redo the time line from time to time, by the way, as long as that person is still in your life, because events will continue to occur with that person in the future. Each time you remap the relationship, pick up where the last time line left off. When you are done, you will see that the buttons will be gone. The person whose relationship you are mapping will not necessarily be any different in the future, but they don't have to be, because you will be.

The next step is to take all the statements you have written beside the vertical marks and write them down under one of three distinct categories.

THINGS I WANT TO FORGIVE YOU FOR
THINGS I WANT TO APOLOGIZE FOR
THINGS I WANT TO THANK YOU FOR

Let's take a moment to focus on forgiveness. Forgiveness DOES NOT mean you accept what that person did, and it was okay. FORGIVENESS DOES MEAN that you are no longer going to let this event hurt you or use this event to hurt yourself.

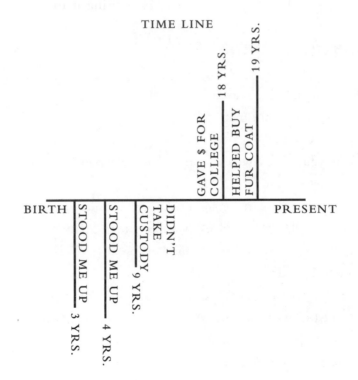

Almost every event on the time line represents an incomplete communication. The incompleteness may be positive or negative. We are just as incomplete when we forget to say "Stop that" as we are when we forget to say

"I really appreciated that." For every incomplete exchange, a button is installed.

In creating the time line, you have probably stumbled on buttons that you may have installed in other people (such as your children). You have also discovered events where something more needed to be said or done. I call it "thanks," but it can be any other significant thing that needed to be said or done.

You may want to sort the various events with colored pens or pencils. But then you will still have to rewrite them under the appropriate category.

Now you are going to use the events-in-categories list to write a letter to this person. The other person will never see, hear, or have this letter read to them. This letter is for you, but you are writing it to them. You will write:

Dear _____,

I have been thinking about our relationship and there are some things I feel are incomplete, and I would like to share my truth with you.

First I want to apologize for . . .

Write each event from the apology category and as much, or little, of your explanation for it as you feel you should.

I apologize for . . .

Do this for each event listed under the apology category. Then move to forgiveness.

I also want to forgive you for . . .

Write each event from the forgiveness category and as much, or little, of an explanation for it as you feel you should.

I forgive you for standing me up when you were supposed to visit me, for my entire childhood.

I forgive you for never giving me any memorable Christmas or birthday gifts for my entire life.

I forgive you for not protecting me from my mother and making me responsible for my own care and custody.

I forgive you for not showing up when I was attacked.

I forgive you for doing nothing when your best friend molested me and I told you about it.

I forgive you for not showing up at my plays or my graduation.

I forgive you for philandering.

I forgive you for not caring for Grandma Ollie in her illness.

I forgive you for letting your wife change my grandmother's obituary.

I forgive you for dying without a will or insurance, and for not looking after my grandparents' interests.

I forgive you for being a Peter Pan.

Do this for each event listed under the category. At the end of the forgiveness statements, write:

I am doing this because I choose to free you from any negative ties that bind us and I choose to free myself from the stories I have told myself which I have allowed to continue to inflict pain upon myself, long after the events had passed. I set you free and, in doing so, I free myself as well. I will no longer speak of these things to myself or others in ways that may cause either of us harm.

Then move to,

I want to thank you . . .

Or,

There are a few other significant things I have never shared which I would like to share now . . .

Write each event from the "thanks" category and as much or little of an explanation for it as you think you need to.

I want to thank you for dry cleaning my clothes when I was in elementary school.

I want to thank you for never saying anything unkind about my mother.

I want to thank you for giving me $3,000 for college.

I want to thank you for showing up to help me organize my life during my divorce.

I want to thank you for telling me you admired me, and for saying that anyone else who had gone through what I went through would have killed herself, killed someone else, become a drug addict, or gone insane.

Or,

I want you to know that I acknowledge that you were a model to me, for being successful and acquiring beautiful things, and you were a model of ambition for me. In you I was able to see a reflection of my own ambition and my desire for better things in my life.

Do this for each event listed under the "thanks" category.

When you have completed your letter, rest. Take a day off. Allow yourself to synthesize all the new circuits you have created. Walk around for a day with this new version of your life. Then come back for the final and most joyful part.

. . .

I applaud you for coming back.

Now for the final part, you will need another person—not the person the letter is to or about. Not anyone who knows the person the letter is to or about. A total stranger would be ideal, but in the absence of a willing stranger, ask a person who makes you feel good, someone who listens to you, someone you feel comfortable being with and sharing your thoughts with. Perhaps you can use a deacon of your church or a prayer partner.

Ask this person to give you fifteen minutes of their time. Schedule it when it works best for both of you. Don't wait too long to complete the process. How long is too long? Don't let it go more than a day or two. If your ideal listening person is unavailable, don't let that take you out; choose someone else. Whomever you choose will be perfect to complete the process.

Find a quiet, empty space and sit facing one another. Tell the person that all they are to do is sit and listen, not respond. Ask them if you may hug them at the end. Then begin reading your letter to them. When you are done, hug them and thank them for the gift they have just given you.

You may now tear your letter into pieces. You may burn it. You may store it in a private place. To be really complete, destroy it and be done with all remnants of it. It is no longer your story. You have voluntarily released it and, in so doing, freed yourself from it.

Do this process as many times, and with as many people, as you require.

Now: Bask in the lightness of a burden lifted.

1. I K T
   I Know That

2. How you do anything is _____.

3. You'll see it when _____.

4. Events have the meaning _____.

5. Genius is _____, while Mediocrity is

   _____.

6.   L _____
                       B

7. Diagram of the tree with roots.

8. What I SEE, I FORGET.
   What I HEAR, I REMEMBER.
   But what I DO, I UNDERSTAND.

9. T → F → A
   Thoughts lead to Feelings, which produce Action.

10. It's what you don't know that you don't _____ that does you in.

11. Prove somebody wrong?

    Prove themselves right?

    Keep someone from hurting them?

    Hurt someone for hurting them?

    Prove how good they are?

    Prove how bad someone else is?

12.

THOUGHT	FEELING	DEGREE OF FEELING
Most rich people are very happy.	Hopeful	30%

13. Upping the stakes

14.
$$NI \to OC < {CS \atop CD}$$

New Intention → Old Circumstance < Choose Different
                                        Choose Same

15.   **F.**   Face

       E.   Everything

       A.   And

       R.   Recover

16. Doubt the Doubt.

FOUR

DESIGN LIVING WITH YOUR DREAMS FULFILLED

Would you like to know why most people never get what they want? Because most people don't know what they want.

Would you like to know why most of the people who *do* know what they want *still* don't get what they want? Because they are waiting for the right set of circumstances or conditions.

C = F
Clarity = FOCUS

Would you start out on a trip without a destination? That's how most of us live our lives. If you don't know what you want, what's your destination?

IF YOU DON'T KNOW WHERE YOU'RE GOING, YOU'LL PROBABLY END UP SOMEPLACE ELSE.

Clarity is your destination, and focus is the road map. Starting out without a map is almost as bad as starting out without a destination.

You may say, "I know I want to be rich." Well, how rich is rich? Michael Jordan "rich," or the-man-who-pays-Michael-Jordan's-salary "rich"? How much do you want? How much do you need? If you don't know, how are you ever going to get there?

And what are the riches for? Nature truly does abhor a vacuum. So, let's say you're clear about how much you want. You will still need to know what you intend to do with it. For if you don't have a purpose and a plan for that wealth, the universe certainly does. It really doesn't matter how much money comes in; if you're standing there receiving an ocean of money without the clarity you need, it will pour right back out like the tide and leave you standing on wet sand.

This is your life. You may have been pushed into it, but once you got here, you were more or less on your own. Your life doesn't have to look like anybody else's life who has ever lived before. Why should it? You're not just like anyone else who's ever lived before.

There have never been two identical snowflakes. Snowflakes, of course, aren't concerned with what other snowflakes look like. So why are you so concerned with what other people's lives look like, when yours doesn't have to be like theirs? There may be parts of another person's life that you aspire to, but why limit yourself even to that?

If it's already in existence, it's a limitation. Think beyond it!

Once my girlfriend Charlayne Woodard and I were talking about great black actresses and their careers: Halle Berry, Angela Bassett, Alfre Woodard. It's a short list, but these are the crème de la crème, the Oscar winners and nominees. Almost at the same time we both said, "None of them has the career that I want." In fact, the career that each of us wanted didn't already exist in the life of any actor we could think of: male or female, white or black. Our ideas for our careers were not like one another's, and they weren't like anyone else's in existence.

People spend so much money to find out how other people got what they got and did what they did. Believe me, there is a great system in that. Because if someone has already done the research, if someone else has already figured out the market, why reinvent the wheel? Be the second best on the market, and learn from all of their successes and their mistakes.

When T. Harv Eker was preparing to open his first sporting-goods store, he checked out the biggest and best stores of that kind and then did similar things to what their owners did. He didn't have to be exactly like them, but he learned from them and made a great living following in their footsteps. It's certainly a way to go. But at the same time, it's a limitation.

If the things you want are the same things that everybody else has, what's the point of your own existence? How are you contributing to the evolution of the planet? There is not one thing in nature that exactly mimics anything else, and yet we, the so-called highest and most advanced creatures on the planet, want to be cookie-cutter versions of one another. The entire marketing and advertising industry is built on our desire to be like others. Capitalism would fail if this desire didn't exist.

Is the meaning of your life to support marketing, advertising, and capitalism? Were you born to be the perfect consumer? Think of that ad: "He who dies with the most toys . . . is still dead."

Nobody gets outta here alive. What are you gonna do with the days and weeks and years that are given to you to be fruitful and multiply within?

Instead of modeling somebody else's way of life, maybe you could become the model for a whole new way of life. Would you like to become the model for a unique and as-yet-unexperienced way of living: *your* way of living?

Then you need to get clear about what you want. This entire chapter is devoted to processes for tapping into that infinite well of possibility.

The Talmud says that every blade of grass has an angel leaning over it, whispering, "Grow, grow!" How much more so for each one of us!

I attended Columbia College writing school. One of the unique things about their program is that when you apply for the undergraduate level, they require no writing samples. Why not? They do not require writing samples because they teach by using a method that they believe can work for anyone. As clear as Columbia is about teaching its writing system, that's how clear I am that I can teach you to create a bigger and better life than you've ever imagined living.

One of the first processes of the Columbia system is to begin writing— just to begin writing whatever comes into your head. Julia Cameron talks about this in *The Artist's Way*, with her morning pages. Just writing down something—anything—is how you turn on the faucet of creativity.

Think about a normal sink in an ordinary kitchen. If you haven't turned on that faucet for a long time, what happens? What is the first thing that comes out when you turn on a faucet after weeks of disuse? Thick, crusty, rusty water comes out, and it stains the sink. But if you keep the tap open, and just run that water more and more, in just a little while the water is running pure and clean and fresh.

You need to be as clear about what you want as that water is clear. So let's start writing.

What are we writing: goals, dreams, heart's desires, wildest wishes, what we are going to be, do, have, see—99 of them. And not a cookie cutter "I read about it, can recite it, saw it on TV" list. First test of any item on the list: If you know how to do it already, it's not worthy of you. It's not big enough! Think again; think bigger. Imagine that: 99 wild wishes! We've already said that the rust has to come out first, so just start writing. Numbers 1–50 will be the rust. It may take days; that's okay, just keep writing until you reach wild wish #99. Then recopy numbers 90 through 99 here:

90

91

92

93

94

95

96

97

98

99

Maybe somewhere around wild wish 90, you started hitting pay dirt. You had exhausted all your mundane desires about paying the bills, putting your kids through college, saving for a vacation, and you started tapping into the crazy ideas that make your heart race. The dream to run a marathon or climb Kilimanjaro, be a race-car driver, finish a triathlon, end illiteracy in your community, end hunger in one village, own a private jet, own a sports team, be a best-selling author, win a Grammy, a Pulitzer. This is where you want to be!

Notice how those dreams in the 90-to-99 range make you feel? Can you smell it, taste it, hear it, touch it? Can you see it? Pick one goal and write down exactly what you experience when you think about it.

The way you feel right now is the energy of manifestation. It's the place you create from. Because in order to have your dreams come true, you must live from the place where they are already true.

Quantum physicist David Bohm talks about the "implicate" and "explicate" order. Take the seed: The implicate orders of the plant, flower, tree, fruit, or vegetable are held completely within the seed. If the seed is placed in the right environment, over time, the explicate order from the seed reveals itself in the form of that type of plant. It is the same with you and your dreams. You are the seed. This conjuring of the feeling of the dream fulfilled is the soil, the sun, the nutrients that, together, will allow the explicate order to unfold.

You and I have not always been able to put ourselves in the right environment. We say we want to be kind people, yet we hang out with gossips. We say we want world peace while we idly complain about all the problems in our country as if they are someone else's problems. We say we want to be happy, but we keep choosing what we know makes us unhappy.

What would happen to an apple seed if it were planted in the Arctic? How many apples do you think that would produce? It wouldn't even sprout. It's easy to understand this principle about the apple seed. But it's also easy to miss that same point about ourselves in our own lives.

Oh, you're thinking, "I don't have the connections/the contacts/the money/whatever to be in the environment that would nurture my dreams."

Bull! The environment is not "over there." The environment is inside you.

When you wrote down the dream, and used all your senses to experience it in your mind, you put yourself in the fertile soil for the creation of whatever you want to be/do/have.

Do you take time to see yourself living the dream? Do you talk to yourself in the mirror, in the car, walking down the street, as if you are already in the world you want to be living in?

Then how do you expect to get there?

Remember: The brain does not distinguish between a memory and a "real" present-tense event. It's all made of the same stuff inside those cerebral cells. Shakespeare said that a coward dies a thousand deaths. That's because each feared and imagined catastrophe is the equivalent, for the mind, of the "real" event. There is no "out there" except the one you are creating inside your mind right now.

How's it looking in there?

Do you like what you see?

Or could your projector use a new lens?

Many of us set goals, or New Year's resolutions, or even make five- or ten-year plans. These are great things to do. But what happens when you've checked off everything on your list? Are you thinking, "Ha, that's never happened before, and is not very likely to happen now"? Don't ever say that again. If you follow the processes and practices in this manual, you *will* meet your goals, and more quickly than you can imagine. What will you do then? Will you make another list? You probably won't know what to do!

Would you like to know the most important thing to do when you've checked off, as complete, all your goals, resolutions, five-year plans?

Celebrate! Congratulate yourself!

This step of self-praise is critical in the success-creating process, and we'll talk more about it in a later chapter. For now, know that it is an essential part of creating the life of your dreams.

Do you know what that celebration looks and feels like? It's a lot like the feelings you wrote down when you were creating the goal to begin with. Most of us set goals, but we never really take the time to focus on what our lives will be like when our goals are fulfilled. That is what you want to do.

You don't want to spend your life chasing goals; you want to live your life with goals fulfilled.

Take a moment now and imagine a place in time that is right *after* every goal is attained. What do you see, hear, taste, touch, feel? Who is there with you? Who is no longer there?

Now take a snapshot of that moment. And as you look at that picture, slowly rise above it, so you are looking down into it. See it? You own it. You have now put an order into the universe. You will come back to this snapshot again and again. Inside this snapshot are all the sensorial aspects of the life you want to live.

Jean Houston, philosopher and founder of *The Foundation for Mind Research and the Mystery School*, said that in her research and study of indigenous cultures around the world, people use as many of their senses as possible to solve problems and to create their world. When a problematic situation comes up in the community, the people immerse themselves in it. They sing it, dance it, paint it, act it out, delve into it in every possible way, to fully engage all their power to focus and bring about a change in their world.

Children do this all the time. Unfortunately, we tell them to grow out of it, to stop acting "childish," to deal with problems as we do—ineffectively, that is. (Aren't we, the adults, the elders, the originators of all the wars, hardships, and misery that are so devastating to children?) I remember my mother telling me that when I was a child, she couldn't punish me by sending me to my room. Alone in my room, I would dream up the worlds that I would love to live in. I reveled in the flights of fancy I indulged in there. At age six, I had a ten-page list of the things I was going to be when I grew up. It got lost somewhere along the way. And just like you, I have had to find it and reconstruct it.

Do you remember the Sears "wish book"? It came out before every Christmas, and was a virtual directory of every toy under the sun. How I looked forward to that book! I would spend hours combing through it with the greatest joy. I played—in my imagination, and as much as I wanted—with every toy in that treasure trove. By Christmas I hardly needed anything, because I had thoroughly enjoyed myself inside the pages of that book as I conjured it all up in my own mind.

Who were you going to be when you grew up?

What happened to that person?

My daughter has inherited this gift in an even more powerful way than I. She thinks of things and they happen. One day her brother wouldn't let her ride his bike and she got very upset. The very next day, a check came in the mail from a relative, and she bought her own bike.

How I hope you have had moments of magic like this as a child, moments when you knew that the world was truly a magical place. But even if you didn't, you can begin to have those moments right now.

And here is where many of us meet our resistance. Place your hand across your heart and say

> *The world is a magical place.*
> *There is nothing I cannot be/do/have.*

What story comes up for you? Write it down.

_____

_____

_____

_____

Did you write down a story that is magical, like my daughter's bicycle? Good for you!

But what if you wrote something that leaves you cold instead of giving you the spark of possibility? Where did that story come from? Is it even your own? Did someone tell it to you—if so, how many times? Did you perhaps witness it happening to someone else? So now you *know* something else that takes you out; a story that takes you away from the joy, happiness, and success that is just waiting for you to be ready to receive it.

Now, what about you people who still haven't written down your list of goals that you want to achieve? What's that about? *Write it down.*

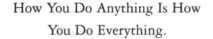

How You Do Anything Is How
You Do Everything.

T. Harv Eker

Can't even make a list of things you want? How often does that happen? The kids ask what you want for Christmas, your friends ask what you'd like for your birthday, your partner asks what you want for your anniversary, and you just don't know?

Well, I have an extremely simple answer for you, for the next time someone asks you what you want. Let's be clear: The situation is not a problem to be solved; it's a moment where your choice has no consequences other than good ones, and still, you can't muster an answer. This is what you're going to do: From now on, whenever someone asks what you want and you don't know, you're going to go to:

M.S.U.

It's not a Big Ten university or even one of the Ivy League schools. But it is the absolute and complete source for everything you need, in terms of desires of the kind uncertain and unknown. My professor William Esper used to tell students who didn't have an answer to . . .

MAKE SOMETHING UP!

Right there, on the spot, make something up. You are no longer allowed to say, "I don't know," or, "Let me think about it," or, "I don't need anything," or, "You choose something," because *That's how you got to the life you're living now.*

You've been running somebody else's programs, living out somebody else's dreams, letting somebody else call the shots. You're reading this book because you want to change your life, right?

You're ready for more; you feel you deserve more?

Then act like it.

Making something up is easy. Knowing what you want is not. In fact, it took me over forty years to even understand what the question "What do you want?" meant.

When I first went to court for my divorce and custody case, Judge Elliott Wilke gave me everything: the kids, both houses, you name it. My husband then immediately took a quick sidebar with his attorney and came back saying he wanted to reconcile. Imagine my surprise! The judge turned to me and asked, "Ms. Pinkins, what do *you* want?" I stood there, silent. I could not respond. I didn't even understand the question. So he repeated, "What do you *want,* Ms. Pinkins?" You know what I said? "Your Honor, I didn't file for divorce. I didn't want a divorce; but if he wants a divorce, we'll get a divorce; if he doesn't want a divorce, well, we won't get a divorce." Some of you are like I was, so you're thinking, "Well, that makes sense." But I did not answer the question "Ms. Pinkins, what do *you* want?" because I didn't know what he was talking about. I couldn't remember anybody ever asking me what I wanted. But I was always aware of what everybody else wanted. And as far back as I could remember, it had always been my job to respond to what everybody else wanted.

What do you want? There is no wrong answer.

M.S.U. really would have come in handy for me back then. But I had nothing to say because I didn't even know I was entitled to want.

How many of you are there right now? You don't know what you want. You don't know what it is to want something for yourself, independent of what somebody else wants or needs.

This inability to access a sense of one's self and one's own desires can affect men and women. It is a common trait of the people our society calls "enablers/codependents." It's not your fault if it has been part of your life.

When you grow up in a chaotic community or a chaotic household, you may be the person who handles it by taking care of everyone. This is a tremendous survival skill. How many lives and relationships have you saved? OK, congratulate yourself. Now, imagine what your own life would be like if you turned even a little bit of that energy toward fulfilling your own needs.

Sounds impossible? It's not. If you've read this far, some part of you is interested and willing. We may have to coax it out. You see, your entire life has been a reaction to what was going on outside, in other people's lives. And perhaps, in your past, this developed to ensure your own survival. Because you wouldn't have made it otherwise; perhaps whoever was "over there" was bigger and more powerful than you; someone you had to rely on, or whose approval you needed. If they were your parents, for instance, if you didn't take care of them, who would take care of you?

And it seemed so natural while it was happening. Of course you don't want your father to lose his job, so you hide the alcohol bottles. Of course you don't want your mother to get in trouble with her boss, so you make the call to excuse her for not showing up. Or you work when you could be in school, because you need to pay the family's rent, or you put your siblings through school, you raise other kids while you're a kid; the list goes on and on. The possibilities for taking care of others' needs first are endless. The habit begins in childhood, and it becomes a fixed feature on your map of the world.

By the time you have done this for a decade or so, you're sure the world works this way. You think badly of people who don't live this way. And when one of these people you help no longer needs you, you may actually resist letting go. After all, who would you be if you weren't the one taking care of everybody else?

That is the question to answer now. Who would *you* be if you weren't taking care of everybody else? Because the truth is: You really can't take care of anybody else. You cannot live their life for them. You can, for sure, throw your own life away trying, but still, the bear is gonna do what the bear is gonna do.

I like the bear analogy because we're not too different from bears. You can train us and guide us, but you can never completely guard against that little ferret of distraction that sends all that hard work and training out the door.

And there you will be—pissed off, angry, frustrated that all your time, energy, affection, and money amounted to this: The bear is gonna do what the bear is gonna do. I hope you do end up feeling this way, because if it worked out any other way, you might actually be so encouraged in your deadly habit that you may never want to quit!

Maybe it takes three or four people in your life to throw all your hard work away before you realize it's not your job to take care of them. What is free will for? Is it so you can tell other human beings how to live their lives? Or for you to take advice from other human beings who may not be doing so well with their own lives?

I don't think so.

Do you want to be free to do/be/have all that you desire?

Then give that freedom to other people too.

I don't even want you to write down your excuses for why you can't stop taking care of everybody else, because they are all lies. I don't want you to reinforce them.

And you know what? You don't even have to stop taking care of others, as long as you can put an equal amount of time, energy, and money into *taking care of yourself.*

Remember the last time you traveled on an airplane? Remember the flight attendant rattling off the emergency instructions? "Parents or others traveling with small children: Put on your own oxygen mask first, *before you try to assist others*"—even your own children?

Think about it. If you're not getting enough oxygen, your brain will start to malfunction very quickly, so you won't be much good to yourself or anybody else. Right in the middle of that noble gesture of saving your child first, your starving brain cells can quit on you and as you lapse into unconsciousness, who's there to save your baby?

It's the same with money. If you give all your money to others whenever they need it, you can bet they're going to always need it, and what happens when they need it again but it's gone? Better yet: What happens when you need it and it's gone?

Mark Victor Hansen said the greatest thing I've ever heard about helping the poor: "If you want to do something about stopping the rise in poor people, don't become one of them."

Sounds cruel and callous. But Mark Victor Hansen put his mind and his money behind that statement: He and Robert G. Allen created a program to help other people become millionaires, like themselves, so they can each give away a million dollars.

> If you give a man a fish, you feed him for a day. If you teach him
> to fish, you feed him for life.
>
> —Chinese proverb

Let your life become an example of what is possible. If you don't model the highest and the best, then you're modeling the opposite of that. Do you think the people you help want to be you?

I doubt it.

My grandmother, Ollie Mae Christopher, was my heart. She modeled everything in womanhood that was good and noble and powerful. She took care of everybody and she never needed or accepted help from anybody. But later in her life, when she got sick, there wasn't anybody to help her: Most of the people around her still couldn't help themselves. As bad off as she was, they were still looking for something from her. At age fifty-six she had arthritis, emphysema, she had suffered two heart attacks, crippling back surgery, glaucoma, and high blood pressure. Her five-foot-two-inch frame was carrying about 250 pounds, and her breathing was not great. Over the years that these illnesses were overtaking her, her beautiful home had fallen into a state of dirt and disrepair. She was driving a rattletrap used car, whereas in her youth and vitality she bought a new Cadillac every year. The house smelled of the dogs she bred, who had now torn up her beautiful furniture because she no longer had the strength to train or control them.

I was twenty-three, living on my own in New York City, working in television and doing well. I begged her to come and stay with me, but she refused. Finally, I found a relative who agreed to physically take her to the airport and bring her to me. You see, by this point she was so sick, she couldn't even resist being carried away.

My beloved ailing captive arrived in a wheelchair with an oxygen tube in her nose. She could not walk. She could barely hold a cup to drink from. She was taking so many medications that they were crystallizing and coming right through the pores of her skin.

She became my project: I was gonna heal my grandmother because I loved her and I could afford the doctors and the medicines; I was gonna save her life. First I took her off all of her medications. I put her on a diet of fresh fruits and vegetables. I brought in healers and masseuses. She was starved and pounded and pummeled into some semblance of health, and she hated every minute of it. I later learned that while I was out at work, she would bribe the neighbors to bring her Chinese take-out food full of salt, sugar, and MSG. Still, after four months, she was back to the Ollie Mae I knew and loved: feisty, cooking her own food, nearly running me out of my own house, forty pounds thinner and ready to go home.

But I didn't want her to go home, because I knew what was best: I knew she wasn't ready. She needed to lose more weight. Her body needed more time to stabilize and adjust to healing itself without medications. I knew that the state of her house, the rot and ruin, would push her once again toward depression and hopelessness. And there was nobody there to get it in order for her, to help her, to take care of her, to supervise her living her own life.

I pleaded, "Please, Ollie Mae, don't go home."

She was my elder, and she wanted to go. And she now had the strength to go. I could no longer force her into treatment against her will, and nobody could take her or put her anywhere.

So what do you think happened?

Within two weeks, she was back in the hospital and back on all her medications. I kept begging her to come back East, and she kept promising me that soon she would. But she kept putting it off, putting it off. The last time we spoke, I told her that if she died, I would not forgive her for resisting me, for not returning to me, for staying there, out of my reach. She was a stubborn woman. I was too mad to speak with her the next day.

I got a phone message that she had died.

How do you think I felt? Devastated, because I had been so busy trying to run her life and take care of her the way I thought was best for her that I had not only not been there for her in her last hours, I hadn't been there for myself, to have flown to Chicago and sat at her bedside as she died. That was something I could have done, that wouldn't have interfered with her living her own life, and dying her own death, and it would have eased my pain.

But I got the lesson: I could not live anybody else's life for them. I have never forgotten it.

It doesn't mean I don't help out when I am asked and when I can. But I respect people's right to exercise their free will and live the life they choose.

Don't you want that for yourself?

If I hadn't been trying to fix my grandmother's life, trying to live her life for her, I might have been more available to share her life with her.

What do you have to share? Stories about other people's problems and successes and the parts you played in them? What will your life be like when you focus on your own problems, issues, and challenges? Sure, there's pain involved, but that's worth it if you can deal with them, get past them, and get on with your life. You were born, so you should be here, and you can do whatever it is you should be doing here, so your future success is guaranteed. It's not too late. It may be hard, but,

> *Anything worth doing*
> *is worth doing poorly*
> *until you can do it well.*

Write that list of wild wishes now. Make something up. So what if it's bad or wrong or stupid? How many bad, wrong, stupid things have you heard from other people? The reason I can write this book is because of all the bad, wrong, stupid things I've done—so many that by the law of probability, I had to start getting things right. Show yourself a little bit of generosity. After all, what's the worst that could happen? You might cry a few tears. You might feel guilt and regret for abandoning the one person you've never taken care of—who is the only person you are here to take care of: you. The good side is that you can start over in any moment. Why not right now?

Write your list.

Now for those of us who have traded in our "enabler" caps—or maybe never had one—those who have an easy time letting others know exactly what we want: Your list probably went way past 99. Bravo! You have already conquered the hardest part.

We all find it so easy to say, "I know that." Then we're faced with questions about ourselves, and we find out how very little we do know. But you should know a lot about yourself by now. You should know a lot about why, although your imagination is large and expansive, the manifestation area is still not up to snuff.

I will come back later to knowing how it feels to live with your dreams fulfilled. That is, of course, the key. You see: Many of us are natural goal-setters. We're task oriented. We make lists and check them off, move on to new lists, and it's fun for a while. But it's also a bit like being on a treadmill. Do you ever feel like you want to get off?

Do you want to have a day where you don't have anything to accomplish? You want to just vegetate, be a couch potato, and watch TV? (Okay, maybe not watch TV.) But you're tired of constantly running from one thing to the next and feeling like you've never gotten anywhere: Ever feel that way?

I told you earlier that by the time I was thirty, I had achieved all of my finest and grandest dreams. And within four months, my world began to crumble; within three years, everything was gone.

You see, I knew how to set goals and I knew how to achieve them. But now I know how to live with my goals fulfilled—and that's where almost everyone falls short.

Have you ever taken the time to figure out what your life will be like when your goals are fulfilled? What will your life be like when you are financially free? What will your life be like when all your future days are paid for, so you can do whatever you want with your time and energy? What will your life be like when you are with your soul mate and you are both on the same track?

There is a story of a businessman who was on a boating vacation and he noticed a guy with a small boat who went out a couple of hours every morning and then came back and spent the largest part of the day lounging on the beach. The businessman struck up a conversation: "Hey, I see you've got your own boat and you go out and fish for a couple of hours each day, but most of the day you're just out here on the beach. Why is that?" The guy answered, "Well, I fish enough to provide for myself and my wife and children, and then I have most of my time to be on my own." The businessman jumped in and said, "But if you went out eight to twelve hours a day and brought in three to four times as many fish, really quickly you could get a bigger boat. Then you could bring in two to three times as many fish and after a year or two of that, you could have several boats and many people working for you." The guy looked at him, confused, and asked, "Why would I want to do that?" to which the businessman answered, "So you could take care of yourself and your wife and kids and have the rest of your time to do whatever you want."

How many of us know a million things to do that will keep us right where we already are?

We goal-setters are masters of the "how." We have stories from experience for everything that happens. But did you ever stop to think that we got those stories from hindsight? Most of the time, when we first set a goal, we didn't know how we were going to fulfill it. We just committed to it and stayed open and aware of every opportunity that led to it. Over and over, almost methodically, we seized the moment and made use of our opportunities and racked up lists of accomplishments. And still we feel like something's missing. Because before the goal was fulfilled, we stressed ourselves and struggled and worried about "how." It probably wasn't a lot of fun, wondering and worrying and hoping, but not really being sure what would happen.

Would you like to know a way to accomplish those goals and bypass the worries?

I often hire my family members to provide child care for my children. My mother's sister Betty is very near and dear to me. She has traveled with me all over the country. She is one of the sweetest, most nurturing persons I have ever known. But here's Betty: She's a wonderful, loving, caring, competent, godly woman who has a lot of stories about what she can and cannot do.

For several weeks she was caring for my children in California while I was out of town. Every day when I phoned, she would complain to me about what a terrible driver she was. She got lost every single day taking the kids to school. She said one day it took her three hours to get home when she was just two miles away.

I asked what she would be thinking about each day before she drove the kids to school. She honestly replied, "How I'm going to get lost again!"

"Try something for me," I asked. "You don't have to believe in it, just promise you're going to try it, for me." She was willing.

I said, "Tonight before you go to bed and tomorrow when you wake up, see yourself getting to the school easily and perfectly. See yourself already there. And really get into how it feels to have gotten there without any detours, straight, direct, and easy. Just see it done."

Skeptical, still she earnestly promised to try.

When I called the next day, I asked her if she had tried my system.

"Yes, I tried it, and I got them to school without any problems."

I congratulated her, but she interrupted and said, "But Toni, on the way home I got even more lost than ever before!"

I had to laugh. "What were you thinking on the way home?"

"Well, I was thinking that I still didn't know how to drive, and it was just luck that I got there without a problem this morning."

Now, my aunt clearly had not changed her belief in her own inability to drive or find her way. But by simply changing her thoughts that morning, about one particular experience she was concentrating on and planning, she had changed that one particular experience. As soon as the thought changed back again, so did her general experiences.

Her thought ("I can get there without trouble tomorrow morning") was more powerful than her belief ("I really don't know how to drive anywhere"). Because thoughts are more "real" things than the objects we touch and taste and see every day. In fact, the most perfect form of anything is the thought of it. People are considered great artists or scientists when the objects they bring into existence come so close to their thoughts that they inspire the observer to glimpse the other side of the invisible veil.

So we goal-setters, we have lists of thoughts of things that we are going to accomplish. But how often does a thought slip in that "maybe we can't do it"?

CT → CC: Clear Thought Produces Clear Creation.

Remember, my aunt Betty wasn't thinking her own clear thought that she *could* drive to school without getting lost, because she didn't believe it. She limited her expectation so she got a limited result. But simply holding a clear thought, whether believed or not, produces that clear creation.

Please—don't take my word for it. Try it and see. The truth is the truth, whether you believe it or not; it does not change. Your thoughts are creating your world. Not just some thoughts, every thought. Every thought about yourself, your family, your friends, your job, every single one is creating your experience of it. However, the *truth* about it remains the same.

But we know we don't control our thoughts. Sometimes our thoughts are thinking us. Sometimes we get them from the radio, the newspaper, the TV, from other people. What are we to do about that?

What are you to do about that?

If thoughts create worlds and you aren't monitoring your thoughts, what worlds are you creating?

Gandhi said: "Be the change you want to see."

You can translate that to:

Think the change you want to be.

Did you ever notice that you can't hold two opposing thoughts at the same time? One thought will be dominant at any given time. And if you want to know what you're thinking, just take a look at what you've got.

So how is this going to get those goals accomplished, those dreams fulfilled, without the worry and stress about how it will happen?

Pray believing and it shall be done unto you.

—Jesus Christ

If you have never read the Bible, check it out. It contains a complete manual of the operating instructions of the universe. If you ever looked at the New Testament, where Jesus was performing all those acts of miraculous healing, notice that he never says, "I now heal you." What he talks about is people's faith making them whole.

The woman who had suffered from bleeding all her life had simply touched Jesus' robe and had a spontaneous healing. The Roman centurion said, "My servant is dead and I know you can't come and raise him from the dead, but just say your word to me because I'm like you, in my community, and I'll tell him, and it will be done." And Jesus said never had he seen faith greater than that of the centurion, who didn't even follow Jesus' religion. What was so great about the centurion's faith?

The centurion thought he could do what Jesus did, and it was done. The woman thought touching the robe of Christ would heal her, and it was done.

What you think always gets done. When you add the act of believing, it is done more powerfully and quickly.

What is the act of believing?

Believing is that place we often go in our night dreams or daydreams where "it" already is so. It's the land I briefly brought my aunt Betty to.

There are times when we can't believe. There are times when our old stories are too big. There are times when the obstacles in front of us are too strong. There are times when we need help.

> Again, I tell you that if two of you on earth
> agree about anything you ask for, it will be done
> for you by my Father in heaven. For where two or three come
> together in my name, there am I with them.
> —Matthew 18:19,20.

The Bible often refers to "two or more." What is the power in the two?

The power of the two is the power of standing in agreement. My thought is powerful, yes, but if I add your thought to it, it is magnified. It often helps to have a partner in believing, a prayer partner, a mastermind partner; whatever you want to call the person who lets you become "two or more." Why?

Because we can't always control our thoughts. We are prey to everything we see and hear, and most of all, we're prey to our old "can't" stories. Every time somebody else's negative thought or our old "can't" story pops in, it is like a stop order on our dreams.

We plan for that big house and conjure it up in our hearts and minds. The universe gets the order. Then we have a thought about the responsibility: Do we really want that? *Stop order!* No wonder it takes so long for our goals to come through, even when we have a clear picture of what we think they are.

Until we are clear of all the old stories and thoughts, and until we make a habit of clearing all the new negative stories and thoughts being thrust upon us, our dreams are on a yo-yo string. We send them out, only to pull them back in the next minute. Send them out and take them back, on and on, while we hope maybe one day they will stay out there long enough to come back to us fulfilled.

It would be ideal if we could devote our lives to keeping our thoughts clear and our communications complete. But while we can't, we can still accelerate the fulfillment of our desires by bringing on a partner in believing.

Oh, it was hard enough to make this stuff up, but now, I'm asking you to share your crazy ideas with somebody else. Why not? Then, when you are not be able to maintain the clear thought of your dream fulfilled, when you suffer a lapse and return to your self-defeat stories, the signal beaming to the universe is still clear and strong. Somebody else is holding your success thought. You can even borrow their faith or lean on their believing until you're clear again. When you combine your own energy with another person's energy, together you have more leverage.

Archimedes said he could move the world if he had the right lever. Nothing is too big when you have the right lever. The lever that a partner in believing provides is—what? Can you guess why, after all this very private work, I would be telling you that now you need somebody else to help you to get the job done?

Well, nobody thinks perfectly or clearly all the time. But the universe doesn't seem to know that. Or if it does know it, it doesn't care. The universe is in the business of giving us exactly what we say we want. And we talk to the universe first with our thoughts.

Now, while we are filled with old stories and buttons and while we're not even clear about what we want, a partner in believing leverages us to getting there faster.

See, your partner doesn't have your stories. So when you tell them you want that promotion, they don't know all the reasons why you shouldn't get it. This week you think you deserve the promotion, but next week you see all the great stuff a guy in the other department has been doing, and now you're not so sure. Then you might think of all the errors you made during this last year, a dozen things! And each one of these thoughts, which runs contrary to your desire for the promotion, weakens or even just stops the signal you're sending out to the universe. And that stops your order from being filled.

Your partner doesn't have that story. Your partner doesn't see that other ambitious guy or know about your past mistakes. The partner just knows what you said you wanted. Together the two of you stand in agreement that it will be so. Hence there is a steady clear signal going to the universe of exactly what you want.

Even when you're not certain and not clear, somebody else can be clear. Somebody else is holding the vision for you. Isn't that what best friends are? We just tell them what we want and they tell us how great we are, and that we really deserve it! What if you transformed that relationship into one that produced results for both of you? Instead of commiserating about what should'a-would'a-could'a been, make a commitment to stand in agreement with one another about what will be.

Then when you forget, you can lean on their believing. Imagine calling up your friend and saying, "That other guy did a better job than me this month, I don't know about that promotion." Will you hear, "Yeah I'm sorry, that does sound bad," or even worse, will you hear your friend go off into a complaint about his similar problem and how hopeless it all is? Instead, you could hear: "But we put in an order to the universe for a promotion!" Your partner in believing could then remind you of all you've shared about what life is like with that promotion already in place. Suddenly you've forgotten all about the other guy and the "can't" stories, and you're back in your dream. The signal going out to the universe is even stronger than before.

That's the power of friendship. The power of standing in agreement with another that it will be done.

I had several years of really bad experiences with cars. One summer, three cars collapsed or were wrecked in one month. After that month, I still had to get another car and, fortunately, the settlement from the car accident gave me a hefty down payment of $5,000 to put on a new car. Now I don't know anything about cars except how to drive them. Most of my previous cars had been given to me or bought from other owners. I had never bought a car from a dealership. Well, when I walked off the car lot with my three-year-old car purchased at 22 percent interest with my $5,000 gone, I felt very proud indeed.

I was proud until my friends all told me I'd really been taken for a ride. Now besides my story that cars fall apart on me, I got a new story that I probably had a big sign on my forehead saying, "Rip me off."

Once I had miraculously manifested owning my own house at a time when I had no job or income, I kept getting an impulse that I needed a new car. My daughter kept saying, "When are we getting a new car, Mommy?" A new car, though, was the farthest thing from my mind at the time. First of all, I never wanted to set foot in a dealership again. Also, I was too worried about how I was going to afford the mortgage payments on the new house, let alone add to the stress. I had applied for a car loan several times before I applied for the mortgage on my house, and I had been turned down flat. A new car was out of the question—or so I thought.

One afternoon while I was at the gym, I got the thought to go back to the credit union, even though they had previously turned me down. After all, I had gotten that house, hadn't I? I was doing my practices, and life was indeed changing before my eyes. After my workout, I drove to the credit union office and headed in resolutely. I parked the car about a block away and walked briskly in. When I got through the door, I saw a woman I just knew wanted to help me. She saw that I had been declined there once before, so she mapped out some strategies to make my application look better to the underwriters. I left the credit union on top of the moon, happy for having followed my gut instinct, and feeling certain that I would get a car this time.

As I approached the spot where I thought I had parked, I saw a car there the same color as mine, but it was not my car. Disoriented for a moment, I looked around, thinking I'd forgotten where I parked, but—no. Then I panicked—maybe it had been stolen! My eyes cast about urgently, searching, and as I looked up the street, there was my car, looking like a big metal accordion, smashed right into the side of a humongous truck.

My car had committed vehicular suicide!

It had somehow rolled out of the parking spot, across the street, and into a parked truck.

Fortunately, no one was injured.

My hopes were dashed; all my old stories and buttons flagged; loss, disaster, bad luck, it all crashed in on me. My insurance was not paid up; how was I going to get a new car now? And this car was totaled, impossible to ever drive again.

But my luck was with me. Fortunately, I had rental car insurance, so I was in new wheels within a few hours. Things began to look a bit better, yes, but the thought of getting a new car was by now paralyzing. I would walk onto a car lot and start weeping and have a full-blown anxiety attack. What would go wrong next? Surely something would!

My partner in believing lived 3,000 miles away, on the East Coast. I called Marilyn in hysterics. Her voice was so calm and collected as she said, "The car is no big deal, I do cars, you are getting a car. I will fly out there and together we will go get the car."

Marilyn flew to California and for two weeks we went from dealership to dealership with her holding my hand. When I put in my applications, many of them said, "Not only will we not give you a car, but we're wondering: How did you get a house?" I was a basket case. Marilyn barely flitted an eyelash. I was turned down by so many car dealerships that my FICO (it's how credit agencies report your credit worthiness) dropped 100 points in that single month after my car was totaled.

When Marilyn's two weeks were up and she was about to leave the next day, I still had no car, yet her faith in my getting one was unwavering. I had two days left on the car rental insurance. There was no hope in sight.

I wanted to take Marilyn on a little sightseeing tour for her last day because we had spent most of our time trekking around being turned down by car dealerships. As we were getting into the car after lunch, I got the insane idea to go back to the dealership that had sold me the last car for $5,000 down and 22 percent interest, but I got that idea with a lot of "can't" in the mix. I shared the thought with Marilyn, who had only a positive thought, and she said, "Let's do it."

I said, "No way! They already know I'm a rube!"

"We're going there, right now," she declared.

As soon as they started checking over my credit application, I felt the strong need to get out of there, fast. I told them I was not waiting around because I'd been through this all month and I was taking my friend sightseeing. "Call me when you have a decision," I said.

Marilyn and I left and spent a fun-filled day in Los Angeles. We didn't think about the past two weeks of disappointments for a minute.

We got home about six that evening, exhausted from running around. The phone rang. It was the dealership. The guy on the line said, "Ms. Pinkins, have I got a deal for you!" All I could say was, "Can you just tell it to me on the phone?" But they insisted that I come in. I was neither happy nor optimistic about driving another two hours in rush-hour traffic to a company that had already ripped me off in the past and was sure to reject me now. But Marilyn insisted that we go.

I walked off the lot that night with a better, more expensive car than any I had applied for that entire month, and with no money down and a very low interest rate.

How?

Who cares how? Wondering about "how" is

Heading
Off
Wind.

I know my partner in believing had a lot to do with it. Marilyn never wavered in her thought and vision of me with my new car. The order came through in the nick of time, and pretty darn quickly at that.

What are you more concerned with, how your dreams come true, or that they do come true?

Do you want them to come through sooner rather than later?

Whether you work with a partner-in-believing or do it on your own, you begin from the thought that it is already done.

Creation Happens Backward.

Ernest Holmes, founder of "The Science of Mind," teaches that the nature of the universe is triune: There are three parts to everything that is or ever was.

Soil	Spirit	Soul
Seed	Thought	Mind
Plant	Manifestation	Body

Which came first, the chicken or the egg?

There is no first and second; the chicken and the egg are one. They are the implicate (egg) and the explicate (chicken) order of one single, whole thing.

We are so accustomed to thinking of the objects and manifestations of life as "what is real" that we forget to think about where they come from. We don't realize that everything that ever was, or will be, already is.

At the level of soul-spirit-soil, everything is possible. How does the soil know what plant will come forward? It doesn't have to know. It works impersonally with the implicate order of the seed that is planted, to allow the explicate order of that plant to unfold. The soil has no say-so. Good soil works for all seeds. Our good universe works for all of us. Our thoughts are the seeds that it impersonally works to unfold as our lives. The soil doesn't ask if you're sure you want sunflowers. It doesn't advise you that sunflowers will deplete the soil so that it might not be able to support next year's seeds. The soil grows the seed that is planted.

To see things in the seed, that is genius.

—Lao-tzu

Electricity, radio waves, the impulses technology uses to transform our daily lives, have always existed. How could da Vinci design flying machines four hundred years before the technology came into existence? Da Vinci saw into the true nature of the universe. He saw that anything we can think already exists in the implicate order, waiting to unfold. If you can think it, the way for it to be is already in existence, waiting for you to choose it.

Mind and thought are seeds that grow because they must. It is the nature of the universe to unfold every thought held in it.

The body, the manifestations, the plants are secondary—afterthoughts. Thought precedes all manifestation. Perfect thought produces perfect manifestation.

Our parents do not teach us this. Our schools do not teach us this. Yet the universe keeps operating the way it has always been operating. It brings forth every thought we place in it.

> Cause and effect, means and ends, seeds and root cannot be
> severed; for the effect already blooms in the cause, the end pre-
> exists in the means, and the fruit in the seed.
> —Ralph Waldo Emerson

How can we change our thoughts?

We change them with practice, with training.

I became a trainer because as a speaker and a teacher, I did not see the results I had hoped for. When we watch someone accomplish a great task or when we hear someone tell us what she has accomplished, we get inspired; we don't become transformed. Transformation is in the doing.

I've been an avid reader my entire life. But whenever I changed what I was reading, that didn't change my life. My life changed when I changed what I was doing. I changed what I was doing with practice. I practiced things I didn't believe, I made up things I wasn't certain of and, over time, I not only came to believe, I came to know, because my life became a reflection of the new thought and ideas that I exercised in my daily life.

The training doesn't stop as long as you're alive.

Everything is growing and dying at the same time. We can train our-selves to experience growth and dying as part of a context beyond duality. In this place, growth and death are part of the same thing. That's our next chapter.

Right now, let's create something—backward.

Choose something now. Choose a moment you want to experience and let go of the "how" of it and go right to the finished result.

Actress and Reverend Della Reese said she manifested her husband that way. Before she had met the man she was to marry, she imagined she lived with him in her house. She set out his plate at the dinner table, full of tasty food. She turned his side of the bed down at night and said goodnight and good morning to him. Sound crazy?

I think that's what life expects of us: a little craziness, a little willing-ness to step out on faith in life the way life steps out on faith in each of us every moment.

Act as if it's already done.

The road to having, instead of constantly seeking, lies in deciding what having is like. Make something up. What will one day of your ideal life—as you choose to live it—be like?

WRITE IT DOWN

_____

_____

_____

_____

_____

_____

_____

_____

_____

_____

_____

_____

1. I K T
   I know that

2. How you do anything is _____.

3. You'll see it when _____.

4. Events have the meaning _____.

5. Genius is _____, while Mediocrity is

   _____.

6.   L _____
                           B

7. Diagram of the tree with roots.

8. What I *see*, I *forget*.
   What I *hear*, I *remember*.
   But what I *do*, I *understand*.

9. T → F → A
   Thoughts lead to Feelings, which produce Action.

10. It's what you don't know that you don't _____ that does you in.

11. Prove somebody wrong?

   Prove themselves right?

   Keep someone from hurting them?

   Hurt someone for hurting them?

   Prove how good they are?

   Prove how bad someone else is?

12.

THOUGHT	FEELING	DEGREE OF FEELING
Most rich people are very happy.	Hopeful	30%

13. Upping the stakes

14.

$$NI \rightarrow OC <^{\textbf{CS}}_{\textbf{CD}}$$

New Intention → Old Circumstance $<^{\text{Choose Different}}_{\text{Choose Same}}$

15.   F.   Face

      E.   Everything

      A.   And

      R.   Recover

16. Doubt the Doubt.

17. **C = F**
Clarity = Focus

18. **M.S.U.**
Make Something Up

19. Anything worth doing is worth doing poorly until you can do it well.

20. CT → **CC**
Clear thought produces clear creation.

21. **Partner in Believing**

22.   **C.**   **H.**   **B.**

Creation	Happens	Backwards

23.

Soil	Spirit	Soul
Seed	Thought	Mind
Plant	Manifestation	Body

FIVE

DIE DAILY TO BE
ALL THAT YOU CAN BE

For a man to achieve all that is demanded of him, he must regard
himself as greater than he is.

—Goethe

If I can show you how to be more than you have ever been in your entire
life, would you be interested in that?

And if I can show you how to multiply that level of growth and expansion until the day you die, would you be interested in that?

Good!

By now we have addressed most of the ways you take yourself out of
your joy, success, and prosperity.

People say "never say die," but I'm going to say it. Don't let that take
you out. Die to live better.

The Bible talks of dying in order to be born again. Now, this is not a religious discussion here, but I know that there is great power in following that advice.

We are a youth-driven culture. You have only to look at the commercials and print ads to notice that most products promise to keep us young, the underlying message being: We may never have to die.

Is immortality what we are seeking, or is bliss what we are actually seeking? Would you trade a single moment of pure bliss for an eternity on the roller coaster of life? You're thinking, "Yeah, if it kept me young and healthy."

To experience bliss, we must cooperate with the laws of the universe we abide in. I've noticed that each time a new study comes out telling us how to stay young, fit, and healthy, just a couple of years later another one comes along telling us how that previous method had side effects that this new drug or program will now fix. After those endless promises to fend off old age and death, after the mind and money we continue to put into it, still we all die.

In many indigenous and Native American cultures, death is a celebratory rite of passage. It is viewed as stepping into the greater life. Many indigenous peoples have been known to choose their place and time of death and then go there willingly, with friends and family standing by rejoicing.

You probably don't want to think about dying. It's breathing down your neck every moment and you're doing everything in your power to hurl it away, to flee it, to finally defeat it with the next wonder drug or program.

Death is inevitable.

And like so many other circumstances of our life, if we don't plan for it, it takes us unaware, and that causes extra suffering. We are incomplete. We haven't done everything we wanted to do, or said everything we needed to say. So the agony of death is not the leaving; it is the burden of all the undone work that will never come to fruition.

In *The Tibetan Book of Living and Dying,* Rinpoche Sogyal posits that we should live each day as if it were our last, doing only that which is kind and helpful and true. That way we can surrender to the great birth into the mysterious life on the other side of the veil.

What if you planned your death—not your funeral, that's after your death—but the actual death? How old do you want to be? Do you want to be in your own home? Where will you be? Who will be with you? Will there be music? Will it be in the daytime or night? Will it take place during a sunrise, or maybe a snowfall? What will this world look like when you leave it?

Just pondering this question brings up a host of fears. Write them all down.

_____

_____

_____

_____

_____

If you're not ready now, what has to happen for you to be ready to die in peace? When are you going to take care of those things?

We are all dying every day. Cells are changing in their grand and tiny ways, and as I write this and as you read this, time carries us through a process we cannot stop or completely understand. I have read that the entire cellular structure of the human body is replaced every seven years. The person reading this page is literally a new you—but one ostensibly still running old programs. Here you are with a brand-new cellular structure from the you of the past, yet you run the old program directing the marvelous new cells back to the aches and pains that formed the truth of those already-dead cells.

We are in the midst of birth and death all around us, and not just in the nature of the flowers and the trees, but in the decay and rebuilding of roads and communities and governments. Each day, each minute, each moment, the march of death is the renewal of everything around us, for out of death comes new life.

Death and life are different sides of one door. Each leads to something more. In all of nature, what looks like death for one thing is the very life for something else. What looks like the destruction of one thing allows for the creation and unfolding of a greater phenomenon. The egg must break for the chick to emerge. The seed must be destroyed and its substance consumed for the plant to come forth. The caterpillar must die so the butterfly can unfold.

What form are you in right now? You can't stay that way. You can't stay a caterpillar all your life. In order to become a butterfly, though, the caterpillar must cease to exist; in place of the legs that held it to the ground, it is given wings that will carry it high.

There is destruction in every act of creation. They are two revelations of the same change. In our consumerist culture, which promises perfect happiness all the time, the good life at all costs, rewards in every moment, we have gone to great destructive lengths to achieve a changeless existence. We medicate ourselves or shop ourselves into someone else's idea of happiness: a happiness that has the right weight, the right face, the right man, the right job, the right car.

Have you found anything in nature that is your version of "right" all the time?

Wildfires are an act of creation. Some seeds require heat of great intensity to force them to break open and allow the life locked within to unfold. (The seeds of the aspen pine, for instance, cannot emerge from the coating of the cone unless fire liberates them.) As we have grown ever more vigilant in stopping and preventing forest fires, we have unknowingly blocked the life of some species of plants, and the animals that feed upon them.

As we medicate away the fiery pangs of what we now attribute to chemical imbalances of the brain, or treat new diagnoses that arise to catch our attention every day, we block some of the life within our own selves that is seeking to unfold.

That is the gift of the dark night of the soul. There are those times—we have all had them—when the pain of life seems almost too much to bear. Perhaps we called it "depression" if it went on too long. Perhaps we sought counseling or perhaps the pain prevented us from fulfilling our daily tasks and we needed medication. I am not criticizing any of these solutions. I am asking you to consider the possibility that in those dark moments, perhaps a new you is waiting to be born.

I have had the opportunity to birth four children with the guidance of midwives, and I have been present at many other births. It hit me once that in every labor, the woman reaches a point where she feels she cannot go on. A mother reaches a point where the strain is so unbearable that she believes she will not survive it and simply cannot go through another minute. Most women speak words of this nature during the birth process.

And do you know what the midwife does? She gets her boiling water and her clean towels and all her tools around her, because this is how she knows that the baby is about to come. The moment that most feels like near-death to a mother is the signal to the midwife that new life is imminent.

All of life is a micro- or macrocosmic reflection of itself. I have found this labor-and-birth image to be a most accurate picture of what occurs in our psyche when a new self is being born. We become disgusted with ourselves; we isolate ourselves; we cry out in agony. And when we surrender to the pain of it . . . we are reborn.

I hope some of you have had the opportunity to experience how a long dark night of the soul can lift in an instant. And it is as if we cannot remember why we were so sad, but we are no longer there and we are happy to still be alive. For the mother, the moment of a natural birth ends all labor pain and even the memory of it.

I have now made it a practice to know that when those dark feelings overtake me, it is my time to be reborn. It is my signal that I am entering a new world, and the old ways will no longer serve me; if I just hang on through it, on the other side is a bigger and better life than I imagined.

If you really want the success and happiness you dream of, you have to get over yourself and die every day.

Every process we've engaged in so far has been a step on the road to death: death, that is, of all the thoughts, ideas, and stories that hinder, block, and obstruct you from receiving the gifts the universe is waiting for you to receive.

But it goes even deeper than that because:

Thoughts that lead to Identification equal Limitation.

Whatever do I mean?

Let's say, no matter what faults you are sure you have, despite all of that, you know that you are a caring friend. You can almost touch in your mind the countless times you have demonstrated your friendship and been praised and thanked for it. "Good friend" is who you are; it's part of your identity.

Or let's say you are not the best friend because there's no time for friendship when you're being a devoted parent or a diligent team player or most valued employee.

Your thoughts, which allow you to identify yourself as caring friend, devoted parent, dependable team player, diligent employee, all limit you from being better versions of the very things you seek to be.

Why? Because every self-identifying thought is also a limitation. The vastness of the universe or even the complexities of the human body are beyond definitive identifying thought. They are in the realm of the infinite, and infinite is what you are. There is literally no limit to what you can do or be or have.

But how can you access this level of expansion—by being bad at what you know you're good at? No. But you can expand by being willing to be a bigger, better, unlimited version of whatever you are. You must first die to the limited idea you have of yourself, to be born into the greater version you can already see in your mind's eye.

This has nothing to do with the concept of being "good enough," because if you start off with the belief that you are "not good enough," no amount of improvement can change that persistent misconception. The thought I'm suggesting you try on is that not only are you enough, you are more than enough: you are, in fact, infinite.

And whether you believe it or not, that is the truth.

People often look at me in amazement and wonder how I do all that I do: raise four kids, teach, act, direct, paint, write books. But there are others I look at in amazement and wonder how they do all they do. I bet there are people they look at in amazement, wondering the same thing. I'd put money on the fact that no matter how good, successful, rich, productive anyone is, they always see that somewhere else, there is more of it.

Isn't that exciting? There is literally no end to the goodies available! The supply is truly endless. And each of us can have more than our share, because each of our shares is infinite.

Such a big concept: infinite.

But what, really, is it: infinite, without end.

Many religions describe God as infinite. But what does that mean? If something is infinite, then it is everything. There cannot be the infinite and then something else, separate, outside the infinite, can there? The idea of a "something else" would eliminate the possibility of infiniteness.

But infiniteness is the truth. It's a truth we are not completely comfortable with, because if God—or the universe—is infinite, then everything in it is part of that infiniteness. That means those we have labeled "bad guys" are also part of that infiniteness. There can be no us and them, for there is only infinity.

The rain falls and the sun shines on the "good" and the "bad" with the same force and frequency. Would you have it any other way? Think about it. If only some prayers were answered or some thoughts were made manifest, how would anything ever come into being? We already know that most of our thinking isn't powerful or consistent enough to manifest even simple dreams. If there was some force that was sorting through and deciding, about the minute and the grand, "this one not that one," how would we ever access the ability to be/do/have anything?

Sure, for some of us it feels like we don't have a chance to realize our dreams. Is that you? If so, you know, you get to choose whether to stay in the same reality or to make a big change. Over here, in this alternate universe I've invited you into, if any prayer was ever answered, all prayers have always been answered. And by prayer, I mean thought: that intensive, personal, passionate thought that uses the best of all of you.

In order to make your dreams and desires come true, in a way that is worthy of your infinite being, the first thought you must allow yourself to "die to" is the thought that anyone else is more or less worthy than you are.

We really want it to be so. We want to be special, to be the chosen ones. And we are, already: If we hadn't been chosen, we wouldn't exist. There is no one more perfect than you, there is no one loved more than you, and this is true for everyone.

Did I like having to believe this about, say, my former partner? Not always. Sometimes it's uncomfortable, hard to get used to. But we have to practice it every day, and especially in those moments when someone is not doing what we think they should do. It doesn't matter what we believe about anyone. We must die to the idea that we are better or worse, or more or less deserving, than anyone else.

A thought pops up into your mind: "Are you trying to say there is no right or wrong?" Some things and some people are just wrong, aren't they? I don't like a lot of things that happen in the world, that happen to my own person, but I still practice dying to the idea that someone else deserves worse than I do. In fact, try this. Next time you have that thought, ask yourself: Who deserves to suffer more than you? If you can die to the idea that for there to be a winner, there has to be a loser, you will be able to transcend the world of crabs in a basket and move into a world that can be win/win for everybody.

Die, die, die. How can we do that?

The first and most important step is to be willing.

You see, before this moment, not only were you trying to avoid death, you did not even want to talk about or hear about anything relating to death. And though death was happening all around, and inside, and through you, you had built up a wall of denial so great that it appeared to not be affecting you. You had your death-shields up.

What if the chrysalis tried to shield the caterpillar from death? Not only would the caterpillar die and the chrysalis rot, but we would have a world without butterflies. Sometimes it seems like we do. When I look on the faces of so many who just struggle to make it through a day, I long to see them don their butterfly wings and float from flower to flower spreading pollen and beautifying the earth.

You don't want to stay a caterpillar crawling along on the ground, do you? You are ready to take your wings and soar, aren't you?

The infant dies to the toddler, who dies to the preschooler, who dies to the elementary school child, who dies to the preteen, who dies to the adolescent, who dies to the young adult, who dies to the parent, lover, mother, father, partner, businessperson, elder, crone. The cycle is meant to go on into eternity. We see it in all of nature, yet we imagine ourselves immune to it.

What is required in order to be reborn into our moreness, to be reborn into our greater yet-to-be? The first and most important prerequisite is willingness. We access willingness when we relinquish the "I know that." Without willingness, nothing is possible. Willingness is not an act of doing; it is an act of being.

To be willing to know, to be willing to grow, to be willing to change, is an act that invites the providence of which Goethe speaks. It is not enough to decide to be successful without the willingness to be all that entails. Once we are willing, all else can be added unto us.

I once got a phone call from a gentleman named Frank at my church. We had served together in one of the ministries, and I found him to be a very open and generous person. Our only contact had been at church or at the service meetings, and I must confess that I found his kindness quite appealing. This particular day, I received a spontaneous call from Frank. He said he was just thinking of me and wanted to call and tell me how wonderful he thought I was. He proceeded to pour out a host of genuine compliments about me, and then said good-bye.

I got off the phone all aglow. My first thought was that I wanted Frank to be "my guy" because of the way he made me feel. I wanted more of that. I had no context for this kind of kindness and generosity from a man outside familial or sexual relationships. Yet this man was not coming on to me at all. He was simply practicing some of the principles we had worked on.

A thought of me came up, and he followed through in expressing it to me. He had no attachment to any outcome beyond the spontaneous expression of love, of love not rooted in possession but a genuine unconditional *agape* love.

I felt really good. Whether this man was romantically interested in me or not, I knew that whoever the next man in my life was, I wanted him to make me feel that way.

Then I was reminded that whatever we want, we must first be willing to become, and to give. (We will delve deeply into this powerful practice later in the book.) If I wanted what this man seemed to have, I needed to be it, to give it.

So I examined what had occurred in the conversation.

First, he had no agenda: The purpose of the call was simply to give something to me without any expectation of getting anything in return. I could easily call to mind times I had given to others either to "repay" them for something or to "prep" them for some future request. This was a completely different kind of giving; this was the soul of giving in its strongest, most powerful form.

Second, he had shared an experience of me in my perfection. There were no ifs, ands, or buts to his compliments. Everything he saw about me was perfect, whole, and complete. I recalled times when I seemed to have "the answer" ready for someone else about how to "fix" something. There was none of that in the phone call I had just gotten. Nothing to "fix." Although I didn't think of myself as perfect, whole and complete, it sure felt fantastic to have someone treat me as if I was. How, I wondered, could I ever make someone else feel the way he let me feel?

I realized that in order to give this tremendous feeling to another human being, I would have to die to some parts of myself that I actually held near and dear. See, I prided myself on my nurturing, critical eye. I saw myself as an excellent adviser, one who could be of great assistance in "fixing" what had been overlooked.

But in order to maintain my identity as the critic, I would have to forgo allowing the other person to experience himself in my presence as perfect, whole and complete. This is hard. I'm a parent. It's my job to point out my children's faults, to guide them and correct them in doing better, isn't it?

Or is it?

For whom do you do your best work—for someone who finds fault with you, or for someone who trusts you to get the job done in the best possible way?

I've found that when someone is cautious about my work, they don't get my best effort. In that situation, I find myself feeling that giving my best would be throwing pearls before swine. Why show off your best so someone can point out the nicks and mars?

By contrast, when someone treats me like they have the faith that I can get the job done as well as it can be done, more often than not I surprise myself and get more than the job done; I fill the job with the energy of greatness. Their expression of confidence allows me to step out and risk being imperfect, which allows me to often step into brilliance.

Brilliance lies in the moment that might not work.

—George C. Wolfe

All of our personal qualities are good and serve some useful purpose, but they are not the whole. If we want to express more of the whole, we are required to relinquish our hold on the little bit we are sure we have.

Einstein flunked high school math only to go on to become the greatest research physicist of our time, the quantum mechanics explorer of all time. In high school, where the instructors were busy finding fault with the way his mind processed information, he failed. Freed by his failure from the judgment of school, his mind soared to reaches that no mind had ever before contemplated. In a certain sense, Einstein died to being a good math student in order to become a genius physicist.

When we desire to be more, we must die to all else, even if it seems to be serving us fairly well.

Never allow your present good
to become the enemy of your ultimate better.

What do you immediately see in yourself that you could die to?

If you're stalled for ideas, go back to the survey in Chapter 1 and look at everything that has a number higher than five. Every one of those ideas about your life and about the world you live in is what takes you out of the life you desire to create.

Try this affirmation:

At the center of my being
I am perfect, whole and complete.

Place your hand over your heart and say it loud. Three times. Now feel the vibration you have established. This is the only truth of your being. To activate being, doing, having more, you must begin from this place. You must die to any and all ideas that deny this essential truth of all beings.

> You have to know that you're perfect. Imagine if a baby started out with the weight of thinking, "I have to learn to walk, it's gonna take two years . . . it would just be too much to even try."
> —Sister Morningstar

We are all that child. We are seeking to express the light of our divinity, the light of all the wishes and dreams that have been placed in our hearts. We must die to every limitation and untruth the world has placed upon us.

Not only must we die to our ideas about ourselves, we must die to others' ideas about us, too. Just as you and I are generous in sharing our opinions of others with them, they are generous in returning the favor.

If you can't trust yourself to tell the truth about yourself, why would you trust someone else: because they are outside of you, because they can "see" you? But if another person has blinders on to his own self, why do you believe he isn't also seeing you with the same clouded vision?

> The appearance of things changes according to the emotion, and
> thus we see magic and beauty in them when the magic and
> beauty are really in ourselves.
>
> —Kahlil Gibran

The deaths I speak of are sometimes very subtle, and may go unnoticed until you suddenly find yourself in new terrain, on a new plane, managing the world with skills you never knew you had. This is rebirth. You cannot educate yourself into it. It comes to you by your willingness to die to whatever no longer serves you. There are no formal classes or inspiring lectures inside you, but inside you is the boundless gestation of continuous change. You practice it by letting loose your resistance to situations over which you have no control.

I spend lots of time in Mexico. I met a couple there whom I just love: They are beautiful, witty, and intelligent, and appear to lead a most exciting life. They are always taking great adventures together. They told me about an adventurous three-day trip they took to the province of Xilitla. They traveled through three terrains: desert, pine forest, and rain forest. They ate acamaya, a delicious local kind of lobster. They joined Indians native to that mysterious world in a boat that went up into a water-filled mountain where they swam and then partook of a feast prepared by their hosts. It sounded magical to me and I decided to gather up my friends, take a convoy, and go to that lovely place locked within the alternate reality.

The night before the trip, my friends and I were together celebrating the completion of a big show we had done, and I was anticipating our coming adventure. But soon, my friends began to pull out of the trip, one by one. Now it's one thing to say, "Sorry, I changed my mind, I can't go." But most of us feel the need to give an explanation when we change plans that involve others. Social scientist Abraham Maslow said the test of a truly actualized individual is the ability to say no without an explanation. The guilt-ridden among us feel the need to give an explanation so grand and compelling that anyone would agree with our decision.

My friends who had decided not to go began to tell me horror stories: One knew a woman who had driven alone and been raped; another remembered someone attacked by bandits. Tales of catastrophe came tumbling out and piled up around me like the debris of a ruined vacation.

It was a gift of grace that on this occasion I did not buy into their fear. I felt serene; I felt eager; I felt sorrow for them, but my own excitement was intact. I told them it was fine for them to stay, but I was going anyway. Then it seemed that a contest arose: The more I calmly said I intended to take my magnificent trip, the more they felt obliged to warn me of the dangers I would face.

In the middle of this, I got a call from my good friend Tito, who had promised to drive us on our trip. He said he could not do it. This was a sign to my fearful friends that the trip was definitely best canceled. But for some reason, I heard myself saying, "If I'm supposed to take this trip, it will happen. Right now it's up in the air."

The women continued trying to dissuade me.

Then, one of these women, who incidentally is the same prayer-warrior who helped me get my car, got disgusted with the heavy dose of discouragement and jumped in to announce with bravado in her voice: "We're going. I'll rent a car. We're gonna take this trip!"

Now this scared me.

Marilyn had never been to Mexico before. She doesn't drive highways and she doesn't speak Spanish. Yet suddenly she was taking over, making this wild adventure come to pass. She made a flurry of phone calls, at the end of which things still stood at an impasse. There was no car to be rented and the trip was still more off than on. But not in Marilyn's mind: She firmly believed we were going.

Then we got a call from the owner of the hotel where we were going to stay in Xilitla. Even though I had no idea if we would actually get there, I wrote down the travel directions he gave me. One glance told me, however, that there was a big discrepancy between those directions and those given to me earlier by the couple who had visited there already. I was rattled; I was assailed by anxiety. I thought, "Hmmm—if this call had not come in, and we had headed off on the trip, we would have been hopelessly lost." In the face of this wiggling doubt, though, I remained open to going and hoping to go.

Unbeknownst to me, I was dying. Dying to my need to conform to what the crowd was doing, dying to my need always to know what lay before me.

By one o'clock in the morning, all the women had left except Marilyn and me. The phone rang; Marilyn answered. It was Tito calling back to say that we could borrow his car.

I was about to offer a comment when I heard her chortle, "Great! We'll see you in the morning!"

Was I about to say, "no"?

Now it seemed I had no choice but to take the trip.

"Marilyn, Tito is notoriously unreliable," I heard myself caution. It was true. He would promise to come one day and casually show up two days later. It's the Mexican way. We prayed on it, content to see what the morning brought. We both asked for a clear answer during the night about whether we would take the trip.

Marilyn and I woke up with the same thought: We're taking the trip. Tito arrived at our door with the car fifteen minutes early.

Now my fear really set in. See, I had never driven in Mexico either. Tito's car must have been one of the first Volkswagen Bugs ever made, a primitive stick shift. I was truly terrified, but I couldn't back out now and disappoint Marilyn. Or could I?

I didn't. I test-drove the bug in the driveway and then we loaded my two- and five-year-old in the car and headed off on the road to Xilitla.

I was pissed off; I was terrified; the car was scary; I wanted to blame somebody. I wanted to blame Marilyn. But I held myself back, I watched myself, because at any point I still could have said "no." But I didn't.

Nothing was lost, though, because immediately the universe presented me with the opportunity to die to the idea that anyone else could be held responsible for me being right where I was. By the time we reached the first filling station, I had let go of blaming anyone and was committed to the journey and to whatever it held for me.

I didn't have to wait long for the onslaught of new experience, because we soon began ascending into mountains and onto two-way cliff-side roads with harrowing narrow lanes. Small makeshift crosses dotted the road, marking spots where others had careened off the edge and died. I was less scared of myself driving off than of someone roaring up to push me off, because from time to time huge trucks came barreling toward us, their monstrous wheels clear over the center line, only to inch back in at the last possible second.

Tension filled me. My shoulders and neck stiffened in terror so that I could no longer turn my head an inch to either side. And only then did I notice that we had no center or side rear-view mirrors! A true panic set in.

I inched forward frozen in fear while cars behind me sped around to pass us, showing their disdain as they roared into the stretch before us—the distance of unknown risk. I trudged along in the little sightless bug, unable to turn, only able to see a few feet ahead to the next hazardous curve in the threatening road.

Then I heard a voice inside me: *"This is how you're supposed to live your life, never looking back and only seeing what is immediately in front of you."*

The universe had obviously been trying so hard to give me this lesson that it had put me in a situation that made it impossible for me not to get it.

I got it.

We kept going. The mapped-out nine-hour drive took us fifteen. We reached our hotel late at night.

I missed the turn and passed it by.

The hotel sat on the edge of a perilous but beautiful cliff, and I had no more courage to try to turn the car around, so I parked the car and we gathered our belongings and trudged back to it.

We slept deeply and soundly. When we awoke we planned our trip to the Edward James Estates, an eighty-acre concrete jungle built in the 1920s. The video we had seen made it look so beautiful and exciting! When we got there, what we found was an extensive ruin. A formerly beautiful ruin: 200-foot concrete walls fashioned into fine sculptures of bamboo and exotic flowers, waterfall-fed swimming pools, miles of stone staircases that wound off into nowhere. I blinked and stared. James was a patron to the surrealist painters, and his estate was his homage to the surrealist artist within himself.

The staircases had no railings and wound along mountains and waterfalls. Marilyn decided to stay behind and wade in the pool. I was so happy to be freed from that fearsome car that I took my children and we started bounding up the stairs. We climbed the waterfall. Several times we came to trails where the stairs just ended. We picked our way through paths where the bridges had long since worn away and we could get across only by walking on branches that could hold only one of us at a time. A bond was forged between my children and me, as I had to stand on one side and let them climb, in turn, alone, to the other. We walked this jungle unaided by any guide. Several times we came to triangles in the road and knew not which path to take. Sometimes I would leave them and try to clear a path, only to find that it led nowhere. In the moments when all seemed lost, however, someone would appear as if by magic, wandering through that dense jungle. Each time I would address the mysterious person: "Salir, salir," and they would point us down the right path.

This was not a popular tourist site. There were no guides. So these people who materialized out of the jungle seemed to me to be angels sent to our rescue.

We found our way through in only ninety minutes; quite miraculous if you consider that we might have been lost on those eighty acres and never found.

Walking on my own two feet was refreshing and invigorating. It gave me the courage to make the next leg of the drive. We stopped in the next town and ate that delicious acamaya, which was more than worth the trip! Then another opportunity presented itself. Our waiter offered to drive us around to the next provincial cities. He spoke no English and my Spanish is kindergarten style at best, but I quickly said "yes," I wanted a driver. And though it violated everything my friends had warned us against, we jumped into a car with this perfect stranger, off to our next adventure.

What followed was one of the most memorable days of my life. He took us to see *nascimientos*, places where a river is being born right out of the ground. He took us to see *cascadas*, stunning multiheaded waterfalls that we rode down in rubber tires. He took us to a world that the rest of the world does not even know exists, and we drank that world in like a potion.

And then it was nightfall and I had to drive him back to catch his bus.

I would have to drive at night. I dropped Marilyn and my kids at the hotel and started out. I kept my fear to myself as I drove on the unlit streets several miles to the nearest bus stop, and then made my way back to our hotel, where I found Marilyn and my children basking in the 120-degree sulfur springs filled with healing algae. I eased myself into the liquid warmth.

I am a major insectophobe. If you see a bug on me, best to just get it off me and not call my attention to it, lest my screams and leaping about destroy everything in sight. Yet as I lay in the hot spring, a huge aquamarine dragonfly flew down and settled right on my thigh, and the voice inside me said, "If you have survived these last two days, you can never be afraid of a bug again." So we sat together in the hot spring, that iridescent winged creature and I.

The dragonfly is the spiritual animal of transformation. It was a sign to me that mine had begun.

My willingness to be with my fear, which in that moment was symbolized by the metaphor transformational archetype "dragonfly," was the key that activated me further along the path toward my own inward resurrection and rebirth. So in the beautiful water, the fear, which had flown to me and landed on me, abided with me.

When we started out the next day to take our trip, we discovered that the time calculations originally given to me by my friends, the wonderful couple, were not round-trip estimates. They did not include the return trip! This was the reminder to me not to recklessly put my life decisions into others' hands. It was my responsibility to map out the return trip for myself, but I had not done so. Now we had to make a trip that would take an average person fifteen hours, but with my driving, we would have to figure twenty.

Both Marilyn and I and the kids had flights back to the states in the early morning. We had to decide whether to try driving all day and night, or just blow off our flights and make the trip in two days or even more. You probably have a sense of who I am by now, and what choice I made.

Having decided to attempt the trip, the possibility still existed that we might not arrive in time for Marilyn's flight. The only way we could make that flight was for me to not only drive faster than before, but to drive the speed limit, and learn to pass on those winding mountain roads. We would be driving at night, which also meant all the big-rig trucks would be rolling on that road, because it's cooler at night so they prefer it.

We made our commitment to try to make it back to catch our flights.

The first leg of the trip went fine. I noticed that slow-moving vehicles in front of me put their blinkers on whenever the road before them was clear for me to pass. Had this been happening all along and I never noticed? Of course it had, but I hadn't I realized until now. My conscious commitment to die to my old way of doing things had activated providence. Now I was aware of assistance that had always been available.

We reached the last major leg of the trip just after sunset. We gassed up and made the turn that was to have put us on the major highway back to San Miguel. After a half hour of driving, however, we found ourselves in a desolate town that we remembered we should have passed by and not entered. It was dark. There were no streetlights and the car had no interior lights. There was not enough moonlight to read the map and we were too afraid to get out and stand on the open road looking lost and reading a map under the headlights. So we just drove on. I knew San Miguel was to the south, so when I saw a sign that said "Sud" something-or-other, I turned down that road.

We spent the next several hours on a dirt road in a vast barren land. No buildings, no people in sight for hours, and no signs to tell us whether we were actually heading south. Somehow Marilyn, who had been a passenger the whole way, began to find it all quite amusing. What was funny? We seemed to be driving deeper and deeper into dark nothingness.

Lights appeared in the distance. Then we could see big movement along what appeared to be a major thoroughfare. We squealed in delight and gratitude. Civilization! Soon we would be able to find our way.

When we got to the highway, we saw signs to Querétaro, which was the way we wanted to go, and a diagram showed us how to get onto the road. There were no lights, though, only headlights of the cars and trucks barreling by at 100 kilometers per hour and more. Unfortunately we couldn't just turn onto the freeway and head in the right direction. Somehow we needed to cross to the other side.

I looked around carefully and cautiously edged the car onto the highway. Suddenly every vehicle hit its bright lights and honked its horns and I knew I had done it wrong. I could see a ditch in the middle of the road and all I wanted to do was get there and stop. I was trembling. I was grateful my children were asleep, and I just wanted to sit in that ditch. Luckily we made it into the middle, but unluckily, I saw that there was a drop on either side of the car that went into an abyss. My mind said, "brake and sit," but my foot did something else and the car careened onto the other side of the highway where a double tanker truck was approaching, and I saw that truck hit us, and I lost consciousness.

When my consciousness returned, we were driving safely along in the far lane on the opposite side of the highway we had first approached. Marilyn was laughing and I was crying. I felt dead. And by that, I mean I knew I had died. I had seen it! But strangely, I felt like I was still in my body, and nothing felt broken.

Marilyn had watched the whole thing. I had somehow left my body, not to return until I was driving us where we needed to go.

Many people on a mystic path experience breaks in the continuity of the ego, which allow their lives to expand beyond anything they had previously imagined. For weeks people who saw me wondered if I was high. I would look out of myself through the eyes of my body and see the world differently. The most frightening part of this experience was the utter absence of fear.

In the following weeks I accomplished many seemingly impossible things, because I had no fear. After a while I became afraid that I might do something dangerous and not know it, because I had no fear. Isn't that a ridiculous thought? Nevertheless, that was a preoccupation of mine.

When I returned to Agape the following Sunday, they were singing a song with a lyric about "blooming on a highway," and I knew they were speaking to me, for I had been reborn on that Mexican highway. For a time I had no longer lived in the world of physical limitation, and my material world blossomed exponentially upon my return.

The intensity of it wore off in time, but then I began to develop the "practices" to consciously recognize when these opportunities are at hand.

Dark nights of the soul can be these opportunities. If you therapize or medicate your way out of them all, you may hold the birth of your new self stillborn in your own consciousness.

The crucifixion and resurrection reveal a wonderful paradigm for what happens during a dark night of the soul: First we are betrayed either by ourselves or by an outside force. Then we are taken prisoner in our own minds, fearing the worst. Then it reaches the point where we think we simply can not go on. We may even contemplate suicide. Russell Friedman of the Grief Recovery Workshop once said, "Of course you contemplate suicide when you're in that kind of pain; who in their right mind would want to go on living in that depth of pain?"

There is a story about a king who suffered from a wound, received when he tried to grasp the Holy Grail but instead thrust his hand into a flame. His injury grew steadily worse in spite of all the physicians and wise men who tried to help him. I'll tell you the ending of this story later in the book, but for now, suffice it to say that his suffering became so severe that he felt he could no longer live, yet he was unable to die.

I've always said that the unfortunate thing about pain is that it doesn't kill you. But sometimes death seems a viable option to escape the pain of our own creation. The pain of abuse or apathy or hopelessness is often unbearable but when we can stay with it, it passes. Whatever we fix our attention on is frozen and immovable in our reality. Let things go and they flow by like the river.

Suicide may feel like a viable option for some kinds of pain, but just as the midwife knows that when the woman cannot bear another contraction, the baby is coming, I know from my own experience that in the soul's darkest moments, the light is only a moment away. But we must have faith that the light does await us. And you exercise that faith by consciously and critically experiencing the pain of your old ways, ever fighting to maintain their hold, fighting to keep you imprisoned in the life you no longer choose to live, and affirming to yourself that you will die to them and emerge to live renewed.

When you "die to" your limited beliefs, it is not the death of your body. It is the death of the egoistic ideas that have kept you from being/doing/having all that you were made for.

The following exercise is inspired by the work of Ishmael Tetteh of the Etherean Mission in Ghana's *"PAIN TO POWER"* workshop. Take a belief that you now hold as the truth, but which you are aware is holding you back from all that you desire, and write it here.

_____

_____

_____

(If nothing comes to mind, use one of the high-numbered beliefs in the Chapter 1 surveys.) Now recall in your mind what your response is when that situation occurs in your life. What do you feel, hear, taste, think? Where does it lodge in your body? Write it down.

_____

_____

_____

_____

_____

This next part will take 10 to 15 minutes.

Allow yourself to see yourself, as if you are watching a documentary, the last time this feeling came up for you and all the circumstances surrounding it. As you watch the movie you are projecting for your own review, allow your mind to continue backward in time to every other time this feeling has come up. Keep going back as far as you can, until you have reached what feels like the very first circumstance in memory that made you feel this way; the event at which you created this particular view of your world.

Now write down the story and your response to it.

_____

_____

_____

_____

_____

_____

Now ask yourself, "What was I trying to achieve by making this response?"

If, for instance, you got angry and decided never to tell anybody they were important to you again, were you trying to defend yourself? If you didn't get emotional but decided to never "try that again," were you being rational, sensible, and reasonable? If you went off alone and cried and never told anybody how you felt, were you protecting the others in your life, trying to not spoil their fun? Whatever your reason, the behavior you adopted and the decision you made about the world were designed to get a positive result. They were designed to stop your pain or help you, right then, to get something you really needed. That's an important thing we all must do for ourselves.

The thing is, now twenty or thirty years later, you're still trying the same solution on a different problem. You still think the world works the way you figured it worked the first time this feeling came up, so you're bound to keep using the same response over and over, even if it isn't working for you.

"It just has to work, damn it!"

That won't make it work.

It is no longer serving you. You have to die to this idea of the world.

Sometimes these events can precipitate a dark night of the soul. Grin and bear it, knowing that you are being reborn.

Now ask yourself: "Is there a better way to get what I am seeking?"

You see, we are always seeking resolution, and we often won't put away or lay down a behavior until we have what we think is a viable replacement for it. So ask yourself: What might be a better way to do this, a way that might actually get me what I wanted in the first place?

Write it down.

_____

_____

_____

_____

_____

And now ask, "What behavior will get me that result now?" It might be a different behavior for different situations. Write it down.

_____

_____

_____

_____

_____

Jerome recalled the first time he had played baseball, at about age eight. He struck out every time he was at bat. He missed the catch that would have kept the other team from winning. After the game he overheard one of the parents say, "They should get that boy some ballet tights, he's never gonna be no athlete." From then on, Jerome refused to try out for any sports: not basketball, swimming, tennis, or even track. He came to me because every time he failed in a job situation, he would go find a completely different kind of job, and at forty-five years old, he was afraid that he wouldn't be able to keep up this routine much longer.

When he remembered the baseball incident after the exercise, he said, "It was always a prominent story in my mind, but this time, I saw how it had affected me. I had made a decision to avoid failure by never trying the same thing again." I asked him what his decision to flee from all risk of failure was designed to give him, and he said, without a beat, "security." But as a man, his habit of avoidance had left him far from secure.

Then we explored other ways he might have used to gain security as an eight-year-old boy. He had ruled out the possibility of continuing to play baseball, hoping to improve with time. He never even thought of trying to practice on his own, or asking for private coaching. There were many other ways his need for security might have been met, but as an eight-year-old he didn't see all that. Now as a forty-five-year-old, knowing that the behavior he adopted in his childhood was useless and even counterproductive, he realized that he had to tackle ensuring his own security in order to move forward in his life.

Some people give up smoking only to become seriously overweight. You can't just drop an isolated problem behavior without resolving the underlying need the behavior was designed to fulfill. You have to die to the belief that the behavior ever worked, in order to discover a way of life that will get you what you truly need.

Jerome realized that getting baseball out of his life did not get failure out of his life. He also accepted the idea that risk of failure, by itself, is a part of life, and not a part of life that can be escaped. Now Jerome has a steady job and he's moving up in the company. Now, when he faces a task that is difficult for him, he works hard to master it. The man who could never learn how to do anything had to die, so the man who could get the job done could be born.

Don't get caught in the trap of trying to make something work just so you will be "right." As you increase your willingness to let yourself be wrong or even let somebody else be right, so you can be free, you expand your capacity, and be all that you were meant to be. Don't wait until you're stuck on a highway in a foreign country. Do it now. Die daily, so every day you can be reborn and even surprise yourself that you are so much more than you ever imagined you could be.

And by the way, Marilyn and I both made our flights.

1. I K T

   I know that

2. How you do anything is _____.

3. You'll see it when _____

4. Events have the meaning _____.

5. Genius is _____, while Mediocrity is

   _____.

6.   L _____

                            B

7. Diagram of the tree with roots.

8. What I *see*, I *forget*.

   What I *hear*, I *remember*.

   But what I *do*, I *understand*.

9. T → F → A

   Thoughts lead to Feelings, which produce Action.

10. It's what you don't know that you don't _____that does you in.

11. Prove somebody wrong?
    Prove themselves right?
    Keep someone from hurting them?
    Hurt someone for hurting them?
    Prove how good they are?
    Prove how bad someone else is?

12.

THOUGHT	FEELING	DEGREE OF FEELING
Most rich people are very happy	Hopeful	30%

13. Upping the stakes

14.
$$NI \rightarrow OC < \begin{matrix} CS \\ CD \end{matrix}$$

New Intention → Old Circumstance $<$ Choose Different / Choose Same

15. F.   Face
     E.   Everything
     A.   And
     R.   Recover

16. Doubt the Doubt.

17. **C = F**
   Clarity = Focus

18. **M.S.U.**
   Make Something Up

19. Anything worth doing is worth doing poorly until you can do it well.

20. **CT → CC**
   Clear thought produces clear creation.

21. **Partner in Believing**

22.   **C.**   **H.**   **B.**

	Creation	Happens	Backwards

23.

	Soil	Spirit	Soul
	Seed	Thought	Mind
	Plant	Manifestation	Body

24. **Ts → I = L**
   Thoughts that lead to
   Identification equal
   Limitation

SIX

DEVELOP A FINANCIAL FREEDOM PLAN

If I can show you how to create financial freedom right now, would you be interested in that?

If I can show you how to have more energy for more opportunities than you've ever had in your life, would you be interested in that?

First, what is financial freedom to you? Is it enough money to pay your bills and have a little left over? Is it enough money to vacation once or twice a year? Is it enough to pay for private school for the kids, or enough to buy the fancy car?

In my world, none of those goals measures up.

Financial freedom is having all your future days paid for. Sound good? Financial freedom is having enough income from passive sources to pay for all of your necessities so you can spend your days doing whatever you want. Would you like that? Can you even imagine it? Or are you thinking, "What's 'passive income'?"

We go to school for a minimum of twelve years, and some of us for even longer. We study arithmetic, geometry, algebra, trigonometry, calculus: All this work with numbers, but we gain no knowledge about how to create the wealth that would allow us to use this mathematical intelligence.

I'm sure you know what a job is. Well, here's my favorite meaning for JOB, which I first heard from Mark Victor Hansen:

Just
Over
Broke

How much do they pay you at your job? Enough so that you'll come back the next day. Because if they didn't pay you at least that much, you'd go get another job. And if they paid you too much more, you might not come back at all. Job mentality is poverty mentality. Now, the wealthy of the world need us poor blokes doing our jobs because without us they couldn't be sitting on their yachts and drinking champagne. And our jobs are important. But nobody ever got wealthy doing a job.

Why?

Because with a job, you only get paid when you show up. If you don't show up, you don't get paid. Right? So let's just say you have a great job, you make approximately $400 an hour, working as a doctor. Say you work 60 hours per week in your own business: That's $24,000 a week. If you work 48 weeks a year, you'll bring in $1,152,000 a year—over a million dollars a year—a very healthy salary. I think most of us would happily accept it. But wait, you don't get to keep it all.

You have expenses, business and personal expenses, what I call your necessities. You pay your taxes off the top. Let's just figure 28 percent, so that's about $323,000. Of course, your accountant will figure out a way to lower that. But let's stick with the straight numbers. We're down to $829,000. If you're working 60 hours a week, I doubt that you'll be making sandwiches for lunch, so figure on eating out, probably breakfast, lunch, and dinner. So figure a modest $300 a week on meals (if you're not risking your health by eating fast-food take-out). There's another $15,000 a year without the wine. Then there's rent for your office (deductible) and the mortgage for your home (not deductible); maybe you have two homes. Let's say your home and office together are valued at a million dollars. With your great credit and low interest, say, on the two mortgages, you're going to pay $10,000 a month, or $120,000 a year. Keep adding in autos, insurance (disability, health, car, homeowner's, excess liability, long-term care, malpractice, unemployment for your staff), clothing, private school, entertainment, utilities, your own medical expenses, dental, and myriad other day-to-day expenses, and that million dollars is eaten up pretty quickly. You can't make more unless you raise your fees, but then you have to calculate whether your patients can and will continue to pay them. Can you put in more hours in a day? Even doctors must sleep. So say, at the end of the year, you are able to save $100,000 in after-tax money. In a modest savings or bank account currently earning about 2 percent, your annual interest yield is $2,000. Remember, over 80 percent of the world's population has never used the stock market and even those who do will not automatically become rich.

Could you retire on that? Not if you're still paying your mortgages and the rest of your expenses. So at $24,000 a week salary, becoming financially free is still a challenge. Imagine doing it on $32,000 a year!

Do doctors become wealthy? Absolutely, some do. But not solely from their jobs, which are merely their primary sources of income. Anyone who has ever achieved wealth has multiple sources of income, and a good portion of it is "passive income," which we'll talk about in a minute.

Financial freedom is having enough passive income to pay for all your necessities.

What is passive income?

When your passive income is equal to your necessary expenses, you are financially free.

You want to know what passive income is? Passive income is money that flows to you whether you work or not; you're making it even while you're sleeping! Would you like to make money while you're sleeping?

Now you should be taking notes. Because what I'm about to tell you about is more valuable than that college degree hanging on your wall, more valuable than your business license, more valuable than your job. We're not ready to give up our jobs. We want to add to them, and here's how.

You want to begin to educate yourself and to cultivate passive sources of income. Remember, passive income is money that comes in whether you show up to work or not. Am I saying that money is just going to come to you and you won't have to do a thing? No. I'm saying that money will come to you, and it won't be based on the number of hours you put in working for somebody else.

Maybe you're thinking, "I already work for myself, and I put in 120 hours a week. I'm still not financially free." Being a self-employed business owner is not enough to create passive income.

Why, you may be wondering, if this is the key to wealth, why didn't they teach me this in school? I don't know why. What I know is that without this knowledge, you will never achieve financial freedom. What I know is that this knowledge is available, if you will reach out and grab it. What I know is that you can become financially free if you will practice the system I'm going to show you later in this chapter. Are you willing to do that?

So back to passive sources of income. What are they? I will write some down, but while I'm writing, you think about it and add to the list.

The one we're all most familiar with is the dividends and interest we receive on our bank accounts. But bank accounts are meant for the bank to profit from, not the depositors: Nobody's getting financially free on what little sums we get from the bank.

You probably have heard of the stock market, and maybe you're in it, but chances are that even that hasn't made you financially free, and ooooh, aaaah, the pangs in your gut on that roller-coaster ride.

I am not knocking bank accounts or the stock market; they are streams of income, but they just aren't the safest or most effective streams. They definitely can be included in your income "Mountains," to quote Robert G. Allan. Allan is the author of a series of books and seminars on real estate as a passive source of income. You can pick up any of them or go to his Web site to find out how to do that. What I want to say to you is that real estate, as a passive source of income, must be:

Positive Income-Producing Real Estate.

This means: The figure that results from your rental income, minus your mortgage, taxes, insurance, management fees, repairs, and any other costs of owning the property, must be positive. Otherwise, it's not positive income-producing real estate, and thus not passive income. Instead, it's a debt, and probably a headache.

Oh, I know you get great tax deductions on your mortgage interest, but nothing from nothing leaves nothing. You don't just want deductions; you want deposits. After-tax deposits.

This has been one of my own biggest struggles. For years, I had deductions that exceeded my income, so my taxes were minimal. But guess what? So was my net worth. Deductions are part of good financial planning, and I hope you have a great accountant to handle that. Charles Russo said, "If you don't have an aggressive accountant, you might as well have none at all."

If that voice of yours is saying, "I know this, I know this, I know this," then let me ask you this: Are you doing it? If not, then you don't know it. Remember, we are here to unlearn. One thing most of us have to unlearn is our focus on deductions rather than on deposits.

Deposits must be greater than the deductions. Otherwise you may pay no taxes, but you will also have no money.

Here is a list of some passive sources of income:

Vending machines	Intellectual property
Arcade machines	Tax certificates
Residuals	Laundromats
Royalties	Campgrounds
Franchises	Positive income-producing real estate
Licensing	Multilevel marketing
The Internet	Back-end sales
Parking lots	Inventions

The list is inexhaustible. You might even create some of your own. So let's talk a little about each one.

RESIDUALS. Actors and other performers receive these every time a program they appear in is rerun or appears in a new market like cable or the Internet. They perform it once, and then get paid again every time someone sees it or buys it.

ROYALTIES. Authors, directors, and music composers receive these each time their product is bought by a new customer. So they write it, play it, or create it once, and get paid again every time someone sees, hears, or buys it.

FRANCHISES. Companies like State Farm Insurance, McDonald's, Mrs. Fields Cookies, Jiffy Lube, and countless others have made a success using a certain system, and they will allow you to pay them a fee to use their system and reputation.

LICENSING. Companies that have created a product or service allow you to sell that product or service in a specific market. Licensing is similar to franchising except it can involve items like educational courses and music.

THE INTERNET. If you don't have a computer yet, get one. People are making millions selling around the globe, around the clock. During the Christmas season in 2004, retailers in brick and mortar shops couldn't even compete with online sales. EBay became a billion-dollar company just by creating a site where other people could sell their wares. What's your hobby or area of expertise? Create a mini eBay around something you're passionate for. Even kids can do this. A Web host can cost as little as $100 a year, and you can be up and running a twenty-four-hour global business. Remember, most of the information on the Internet is recycled and packaged from other sources. Know an area where there is very little or difficult-to-find information? Get rich by becoming the source for that area.

PARKING LOTS. A parking lot in a prime area with a drop box for payments can make big bucks. Oh, don't grumble that people won't pay, because the rate of payment for this type of business, which uses the "honor system," is about 95 percent. For the cost of the lot and the box you have a twenty-four-hour, virtually employee- and maintenance-free source of passive income. Just stop by and collect.

VENDING MACHINES. The candy and water machines at your office or school are a great source of passive income. The machines can be bought or rented. You choose the items they carry. You fill them and then periodically collect your revenues. Perhaps you know of a spot where you hang out, where people would buy snacks or drinks if a machine were standing there offering them?

ARCADE MACHINES. Like vending machines, arcade game stations provide passive income. They may have higher maintenance requirements, but that might be a fair trade-off for the fact that you don't need to fill them with any products.

LAUNDROMATS. Those warehouses lined with the essential machines every apartment dweller needs to use. For the cost of the machines and their maintenance, you have a source of income that is flowing in around the clock. At two and three dollars a load, just add it up.

CAMPGROUNDS. Has anybody left you some unimproved land in an out-of-the-way location? Don't know what to do with it? Turn it into a campground and operate it on the honor system the same way as the parking lot.

POSITIVE INCOME-PRODUCING REAL ESTATE. If the rent is not higher than the total cost of mortgage and maintenance, the cash flow isn't positive. A good rate of return is between 5 percent and 10 percent.

MULTILEVEL MARKETING. Many of these businesses have gotten a bad rap because a few are in fact pyramid schemes in which only the people at the top, or those who enter at the beginning of the system, make money. However, there are some exceptions: Isagenix, Amway, and certain others provide excellent service and value. The key in multilevel marketing is still that you make money from the people down your line. So your focus is less on selling your product than on training the people in your line to be the best trainers of other people, so your line builds with great trainers and sellers of a product that, ideally, adds value to people's lives.

BACK-END SALES. Ever wonder how so many companies and trainers can offer things for free? It's because of back-end sales. A back-sales system works like this: You go to a place that has a lot of fish, and you give them something of value for free. The fish who are interested in what you have to offer bite and come down your funnel to purchase more of your merchandise, be it books, tapes, videos, CDs, or whatever. This method cuts out marketing costs. You give away something of value and in exchange create your entire client base.

INVENTIONS. Did you know that the man who invented the aluminum wrapping on chewing gum became a multimillionaire and left millions to his descendants? Inventions don't need to be as grand as the electric lightbulb. We all notice problems with the way things work. Be the one to solve a common problem, and make a fortune doing it.

INTELLECTUAL PROPERTY. Patents, trademarks, copyrights. Anything you think of using in a specific and unique way, and that other people can pay you to use.

TAX CERTIFICATES. You won't hear about this one from your broker because this is a noncommissionable investment. And it's how banks maintain their wealth. You see, all municipalities require taxes in order to run.

Tax revenue pays for services like police, fire, garbage pickup, street cleaning, and so forth. It pays to run the government. If people stopped paying
their taxes, the municipality would be bankrupt and services would have
to stop.

Well, some people don't, or can't, pay their taxes. So the municipality
tacks on a penalty. The penalty is in the form of interest, which varies from
16 percent in Illinois to 54 percent in Michigan. So when a taxpayer finally
remembers, or can finally afford, to pay the taxes due, there's this big chunk
added on, for the late penalty. Well, the government can't risk allowing too
many people to fall behind in their taxes, because the revenue is essential to
day-to-day life. So what does the municipality do?

You're going to love this.

They let somebody else pay the late taxes. It's called a tax certificate.
Let's say Sally goes down to the tax assessor's office and sees a property in
the Illinois neighborhood where she grew up. She knows the house, knows
the value of the neighborhood. The house last sold for $300,000. The own-
ers are one year behind, and the tax owed amounts to $3,000. A penalty of
16 percent accrues every six months, so the owners owe not only the back
taxes of $3,000 but also the $480 in tax penalty for the first six months and
another $480 penalty for the next six months.

Sally pays the tax bill, and for doing so receives a tax certificate. The
owners of the house will probably pay their back taxes plus penalty—
$3,000 in tax plus $960 in interest—rather than lose their $300,000 home;
they just can't do it immediately. When they do pay, the entire interest
payment goes to the purchaser of the tax certificate—so Sally makes $960
per year for doing nothing more than owning that tax certificate. What
could be easier? If you buy tax certificates, the government collects the
taxes and writes a check to you for the amount you initially paid, plus the
high rate of interest.

This is how banks stay rich. They use your money and invest in certificates that give extremely high rates of interest, and then they give you back
a tiny rate of interest for the privilege of using your money. But you don't
need the middleman. You can buy the certificates yourself with the money

you would have otherwise put into the bank, so you get that high interest rate for yourself. There are many varieties of certificates and they work differently from state to state. In California, for instance, you can end up owning the property if someone falls delinquent in their taxes.

A great start for more information on this, the best and easiest source of passive income, is the book *The 16% Solution* by Joel S. Moskowitz.

By now, your head may be reeling. "It's too much information, too much trouble, too much work." What's coming up for you? Write it down.

_____

_____

_____

_____

So now you know why you don't try what you have never tried before, or do what you've never done before.

Whatever you wrote is the reason most of this information has been banished to the land of "heard it, read about it, seen it on TV." Because everything I've laid out for you is a lot less work than showing up at a *job* forty to sixty hours a week.

You know what a rich person's job is? Managing his or her money. She gets up and checks her stocks and calls her brokers and real estate managers. She may go out and collect her cash. And what does she spend the rest of her day doing?

Whatever she wants to do!

Your resistance, fear, or whatever comes up, is just a sign that you are growing. You are moving out of the old way of doing things—which has got you where you are now—because you want more, and you're ready for more now.

Einstein said, *"You can't solve the current problem with the same thinking that created it."*

If you knew how to get what you wanted, you'd already have it. So chances are, what I'm telling you is part of what you need to know.

What would you think of someone who told you they were passing up the opportunity to become wealthy and successful the way millions of other people had already done? Don't let that be you.

Are you ready for the system?

Yes, or Yes?

Are you ready to move out of *job* mentality to financial freedom mode?

Yes, or Yes?

Good.

Here are your six bank accounts, going forward: FFF, MPF, EDU, DON, FUN, and EXP.

FFF (FINANCIAL FREEDOM FUND). This is the most important fund because it's going to be your goose that lays the golden eggs.

Starting today, you're going to begin putting 10 percent of everything you have and of everything that comes to you into this account. And you are never going to spend this account during your lifetime. You're going to invest it, and it's going to grow. And if you like, after you've become financially free, you can go ahead and spend the "golden eggs" that come in the form of dividends.

Yes, I did say this was an account that you were going to keep adding to and never spend during your entire lifetime; it wasn't a typo. What kind of insanity is this?

You want financial freedom, with all your future days paid for? Say you get toward the end of your life and you come down with an incurable illness. You decide you must spend all your FFF. Then they discover the cure! Are you going to say, "Let me die, because I have no money left?"

There's an ad campaign for a brokerage house that says "Which dies first, you or your money? Let's get to work." You don't want your money to ever die. In fact, you want to leave it in foundations, give it to charities or to descendants, so that it will become your legacy.

Suze Orman, and almost every other financial adviser, will tell you to "pay yourself first." But we're going the extra step, because our focus is now on financial freedom and passive income. We are taking the first of our fruits—10 percent right off the top—and placing it in an account to invest and leave to the future.

You get a hundred dollars; where does the first ten go? You get fifty dollars, how much goes into the FFF? Ten percent of all income, bonuses, gifts, inheritances, and every other form of in-flow of money will now fund your FFF.

I download the billionaires' list every year. Two years ago, Bill Gates's worth dropped 25 percent from the previous year. And you know what? He was still a billionaire! Maybe you don't require billions. But what we're talking about is creating a level of wealth that is immune to the unpredictable forces of politics, nature, or the times we live in. That amount, naturally, is different for each of you.

George was a NASA engineer. He lived a very high life and had a home that increased from the value of $200,000 he had paid for it to nearly $800,000. Though George loved his job, he had recently had a cancer scare and he realized there was a lot of traveling he wanted to do soon, in case he died young.

George lived alone in this 5,000-square-foot house. He realized he could easily downsize to a smaller house, but what he really wanted was to have enough income to last the rest of his life. Already in his late forties, George was just learning about the financial freedom system. But he wasn't a NASA engineer for nothing, for he quickly put his brain to figuring that, if he sold his house for $700,000, and paid off the mortgage of $100,000, he would have $600,000 left to use for travel, investment, or both.

George's expenses without the house were about $50,000 a year. So in order for him to walk away from his six-figure NASA salary and afford to travel, he needed to generate $50,000 a year in passive income. So what did he do? He sold the house, paid off the mortgage, and had $600,000 to show for it. He then took $500,000 from the profit and invested it by becoming a mortgage lender himself. He bought a building of four small condos and he financed the purchasers of the apartments, becoming the mortgage lender for his own building. The thirty-year mortgages he acquired paid him 10 percent, giving him $50,000 a year in income. And he still had that hundred grand to play with on the spot.

George simply rearranged the asset he had, the equity in his big home, by turning it into working money, in the form of a secured, safe loan on which other homeowners would pay him interest. And now that he was going to travel, he didn't need his car and health club membership anymore, which dropped his expenses to about $40,000 a year. So now for George, his passive income of $50,000 exceeded his necessities of $40,000, so he was financially free.

You can create your own version of that. It starts with the FFF. Ten percent of everything that comes in goes into this account first.

MPF (MAJOR PURCHASES FUND). Ten percent of every dollar that comes in goes into this account as well. Now this account is, as the title says, a "purchasing account." (You'll be happy to know that all the rest of the accounts are going to be spending accounts.) This account will be used to pay for big-ticket items like cars or home appliances. From now on, when a big expense comes up, you've already created the funds to pay for it. No more scrounging around, begging and borrowing, or living off the credit cards. You have managed your money to account for items that are an important part of life but don't come up on a daily basis.

EDU (EDUCATION FUND). You will put 10 percent of everything that comes in into this fund. Sometimes, getting ahead does mean knowing more. You are managing your money so you don't miss out on any opportunity, because you can't afford the training. It can also be used to educate your children or your partner. Now lack of the proper education will never be an excuse for not getting what you want.

DON (DONATION FUND). I like to tell the story of the minister who went with his son to preach at a new church. When they walked into the modest building, they saw a box in the back for tithes and offerings. The minister had only $20, and he put it all in the box. The congregation was very small but appreciative of his sermon. At the end of the evening, the presiding minister of the church said to the guest minister, "We are a small congregation and we don't have much, but we can give you everything from our offering box." When they opened the box, all that was inside was the $20 the guest minister had put in there himself; he accepted it gratefully. As he and his little boy left the church, his son said to him, "You see there, Dad, if you'd have put more money in that box, you would have got out more!"

You put 10 percent of your money into the donations fund because we can truly only receive that which we give. This fund can be given to a charity, used to support a cause, or given to a spiritual teacher or even to a friend in need. The point is to recognize how much grace is involved in all our lives, and always to be prepared to give back as freely as we have been given to.

FUN (FUN AND GAMES FUND). The purpose of this fund is to use it to enjoy yourself, and to do things for yourself as rewards for all your hard work and discipline in managing your money. This fund also gets 10 per-cent. It must be spent frivolously, on something that has no other purpose than to give you joy. If you like bubble gum and you've saved one dollar in the play fund, buy yourself ten pieces of bubble gum and savor every one. The FUN fund cannot be spent on anything logical or reasonable or on any-thing you need, unless what you need is a good fun time.

So up to this point, we have five funds that we have divided our money into: 10 percent FFF; 10 percent MPF; 10 percent EDU; 10 percent DON; and 10 percent FUN.

That's 50 percent of our income, after taxes. (Always pay the taxman first, because that money is not yours.) But we still have 50 percent left. Where does it go?

EXP (EXPENSES FUND). The remaining 50 percent of your money goes into the Expenses Fund, which pays for the day-to-day expenses of life: rent, utilities, food, transportation, medical care. Anything not in the category of the other five accounts is paid for from the EXP Fund.

When I began using this system, I was on welfare. My necessities exceeded my income by about 1,000 percent. Yet I took my $465 a month and divided it into six paper bags. Of course, I was never sure it would work, at that time in my life.

Sandra Morningstar is a nun and hermitess who has created a new order in the Catholic Church devoted to sacred birth. She resides on the "Holyland" in the Ozarks of Missouri, where she devotes herself to simple and sacred living and service to her community. I met her in Mexico, and she became my spiritual teacher.

One day when I was in the most doubt, Sister Morningstar recalled to me the scripture that advises: "Do not worry about tomorrow." That day, I went looking in the cupboard, and this is what I saw: a can of peas. I checked the fridge, where I found a few tablespoons of applesauce and some leftover meat. So I made a feast. Normally I would have divided that into three meals, but this day, I sat down with my two children and we ate it all. I trusted that pointing my sail toward shore, by starting the financial freedom system, was going to work. I didn't know how, but I knew we would have a meal tomorrow because I was now putting my energy into not just eating today, but toward knowing that eating would never be an issue for us again.

My kids loved that meal. Whereas I would normally have felt guilty about so scrawny and non-nutritious a dinner fare, they complimented me, and I have to tell you, they still ask me to make that dinner again.

The next morning a neighbor stopped while driving by, and gave me $25. I was amazed. She said she wasn't even sure why she did it: She just knew she had to. That same week, I was offered a teaching job that became the impetus for the work I am writing about now. The next month, I was off welfare because my income had increased so greatly that I no longer qualified—and that rising trend still continues.

Let me say another thing: As work—and more—began to pour in, there was a period of about six months when I forgot to follow the system. There was so much coming in, and I was so busy, I didn't have time to think about it. When I finally got a break and checked in on my bank account, it was overdrawn. I was making more money than I'd ever made in my life, yet my checks were bouncing. And believe me, I hadn't had time to do any traveling or buy any luxury items. I was knocking myself out working around the clock, yet all this wealth that had poured in had poured right back out again. The very next day, I sat down, called the bank, and set up six bank accounts. You see, the money had been coming in so fast that I was still using the paper-bag system. (Well actually, I had upgraded to some plastic colored boxes.) But I opened the bank accounts: FFF, MPF, EDU, DON, FUN. I kept my previous bank account for EXP.

Now my necessities had greatly increased, as had my income. They were now almost as much as my total income, and I didn't know how I was going to stop that. But I knew that this system had gotten me here, and I knew it could still turn things around for me.

When I received the next paycheck, I transferred funds into each of the six accounts, and by the end of the month I had put away almost half of what was coming in. After doing this, I found a way to reduce what I had considered "necessities." My money has continued to grow as I have continued putting my energy into the system.

Most of us have a streak of kindness and generosity flowing through our veins—at least toward children. Now imagine, you take your child (or niece or grandchild or cousin) into an ice cream parlor and buy them a big single scoop of ice cream. (My favorite is pink bubble gum.) You're walking out of the store watching their eyes shine as they lick the ice cream, when uh-oh, suddenly they slip, and the ice cream is on the ground! Where there was once a beaming ray of sunshine, the storm has come; the rains are pouring as they cry out over the loss of their delicious treat. Most of us would probably comfort them and tell them accidents happen, and then take them back for another scoop.

So now, you're heading back in and the person in front of you has a big triple scoop. The little child's eyes widen; it's just the most exciting thing they've ever seen. Little hands tug at you. "Would you, could you, *please,* get me a triple scoop?"

Would you?

Probably not, though I'm sure each of you has your own reason why you would not buy the triple scoop. The decision is rooted in a principle or law of the universe. Later on I'll talk about many ways to make this law work in your life, but for now, just consider this—the child couldn't manage to hold on to a single scoop of ice cream. What is the likelihood of him holding on to a triple scoop? Not very good. And you've already witnessed the tears and feelings of failure at having dropped that first scoop. Wouldn't it be rather cruel to set him up for an even bigger failure? You may not have thought of it that way, but in your wisdom, you recognize that one scoop is enough for now. You know that once he successfully manages a single scoop, he then can move up to a double, and then a triple. But if he got the triple now and failed, first of all, he would have tripled his chance of failing.

The universe is benevolent like that. The universe will never give you more to manage than you can handle. Put it this way: If you aren't managing the little money (or the no money) you have right now, the universe will not give you more.

The financial freedom system is about demonstrating your ability to handle the single scoop of ice cream so you can move on to the double and the triple. With every level of wealth and success comes a greater challenge. The ones who rise to the highest levels have successfully managed the challenges of the levels below. By "managed," I do not mean "caused to disappear."

The amount of money in the funds is not the point. You can begin these funds with one dollar or one dime or one penny. The point is to begin to manage what you have, as a demonstration to the universe that you are ready for more. You've got to handle the single scoop before you get a chance at the triple.

Now I have laid out for you a system, a proven way of doing things that works. Yet I know many of you will not even begin it, while others will try to adjust it or improve it and fail, and then blame the system. Some of you—congratulations in advance—will succeed beyond your wildest dreams.

Yet if you will do what most people won't do, for a little while, you will be able to do what most people will never be able to do, forever. The system for financial freedom is a way of doing things that works. It works the way McDonald's, Mrs. Fields, Wal-Mart, eBay, and dozens of other systems have worked, to make their founders immensely wealthy.

So for the group of you who want to "fix" or adjust the system, I'd bet that a lot of systems haven't worked for you. You know why? Because if you fix it or change it, it's no longer the same system. Every one of these categories—major spending, education, fun, donation—comes up in your life. You never know exactly when you'll need the money. You demonstrate your ability to manage money by preparing for the inevitable in advance. If you changed the percentages or increased some funding while decreasing others, you'd be living like you already are, robbing Peter to pay Paul all over again. This system is preparation for all your future days and expenses to be paid for in advance.

The only place where the percentage will be more than 10 percent will be in your Financial Freedom Fund, because you will be tossing your pocket change into that cup at the end of every day. I tell you what: You can fix the system when, and only when, you have become financially free, following it the way it's already worked for others. When you are financially free, in fact, fix the system all you like, because you will have plenty of time on your hands to do so.

What about those of you who won't even try it? I'll bet that a good portion of you won't try it because it doesn't make sense to you. There's no reason or logic you can explain to others for all the paperwork of six accounts and different checks and bank cards. So rather than feel foolish, you stick to what you've been doing, which hasn't been working, until you find something else that seems to make sense, and you'll follow that whether it works or not because you'd rather be right than happy. You'd rather be right than rich.

Your bottom line is that if you don't understand it, you can't commit to it. For you to commit, you need to know *how* a thing works.

The interesting thing is that you don't know how half the things you use in your daily life work—your PDA or your car, for example—but that doesn't stop you from reaping their benefits. Yet when it comes to creating financial freedom—the one thing that may allow you to do everything your heart desires—you cringe. Is it too simple? Is it too hard? Six accounts: one for expenses, one for major purchases, one for education, one for giving, one for fun, and one for your valuable financial freedom.

I'm not much of a sailor, but oh, I love going out on a sailboat. I've taken out a few catamarans and I marvel at how the slightest movement can steer you in a different direction, but when the wind is hitting the sail at just the right angle, you glide through the water without effort. One time I was sailing and a storm began to brew. I love a good storm, but not when I'm out at sea in a little boat. I could see the heavy gray billowy clouds and I began to steer back toward shore, but because of the storm, my efforts seemed to send me farther away from my destination. The winds were whisking and changing almost every second, and after an intense struggle my muscles were sore and I was out of breath and bruised. I didn't know how I was going to get back, but I knew the wind would have to get me there, and I knew that all my changes of course were getting me nowhere. So I set my sail in the direction it needed to be in for the wind to catch it and bring me to shore. I didn't know when or how that would happen, but I knew it was my best choice.

You know what? I was eventually blown safely in to shore. When I landed and was sitting safely with a cup of tea, it hit me that most of us are like I was in that sailboat, changing directions, trying to catch the elusive wind of fortune. Most of us also spend our time and effort on activities that are just like what I was doing: frantically tugging that sail, pushing and pulling, trying to get in control of the boat in the storm. While we desperately try to harness huge forces to move us in the direction we long for, we have no understanding of those forces. We don't know how the wind is going to get us home; when, if ever, it will work out just right; or if our efforts are helping or hurting. When I finally set my sail in the direction I wanted to go, and trusted the wind to catch it and to push me where I needed to go, I allowed my boat to be carried safely in. I didn't do this by plan; I did it because I had exhausted myself, and finally I realized it was my only way. I had to give up knowing how, in order to be taken exactly where I had to go.

Most of us have spent our lives heading off wind from the financial freedom we desire. This system is like pointing your sail and trusting that the wind must catch it and bring you safely to shore.

Penny followed the system and began to create a big name for herself in the field of welding, so big a name that other companies began calling her and accusing her of stealing their ideas. Some threatened to sue her. Penny's first response was to want to reject her success. Who would want to be threatened or sued? I asked Penny, "When you were doing this in your garage for no money, did anybody try to sue you or accuse you of anything?" No. I asked, "Did you have a lot of business then, were many people aware of you or your work?" She had to answer "no" to that, as well. I asked her to recall the lawsuits against Bill Gates, Oprah Winfrey, and various newspapers.

I asked "Did it put them out of business?" "Of course not," she replied.

Exactly my point: As you continue to manage your money and create success, people will want what you have. Some people aren't going to be very nice about trying to get it. With some people, you may feel guilty about not giving it to them. But what goal would be served by your giving it all away just to avoid the pressure?

So you must come to realize that managing wealth and success involves managing all the other things that come with it: guilt, jealousy, self-doubt, even lawsuits. I taught Penny exercises to allow her to expand her identity to include these challenges as a normal part of her newfound success. I taught her to expect that as her business expanded, the challenges would get bigger, and that she would—and could—manage those larger challenges as well. They don't go away. You manage them the way you are now about to manage your money, so you can create more money to manage.

Stand up. Put your hand over your heart and in your strongest, deepest voice, say:

I Am Financially Free.
New Challenges Are No Obstacle to Me.

Repeat it. Sing it. Dance it.

Now be still, and feel the vibration of your body. Notice the change in the atmosphere in the room. This is the vibration of wealth and financial freedom. You are creating it now. What thoughts occur to you? Write them down:

_____

_____

_____

_____

So, get up and go divide your money into those paper bags.

1. I K T

   I know that

2. How you do anything is _____.

3. You'll see it when _____.

4. Events have the meaning _____.

5. Genius is _____, while Mediocrity is

   _____.

6.   L _____

                      B

7. Diagram of the tree with roots.

8. What I *see*, I *forget*.
   What I *hear*, I *remember*.
   But what I *do*, I *understand*.

9. T → F → A
   Thoughts lead to Feelings, which produce Action.

10. It's what you don't know that you don't _____that does you in.

11. Prove somebody wrong?

    Prove themselves right?

    Keep someone from hurting them?

    Hurt someone for hurting them?

    Prove how good they are?

    Prove how bad someone else is?

12.

THOUGHT	FEELING	DEGREE OF FEELING
Most rich people are very happy.	Hopeful	30%

13. Upping the stakes

14.
$$NI \to OC < \begin{matrix} CS \\ CD \end{matrix}$$

   New Intention → Old Circumstance $< \begin{matrix} \text{Choose Different} \\ \text{Choose Same} \end{matrix}$

15.
F.	Face
E.	Everything
A.	And
R.	Recover

16. Doubt the Doubt.

17. **C = F**
    Clarity = Focus

18. **M.S.U.**
    Make Something Up

19. Anything worth doing is worth doing poorly until you can do it well.

20. **CT → CC**
    Clear thought produces clear creation.

21. **Partner in Believing**

22.   **C.**   **H.**   **B.**
        Creation   Happens   Backwards

23.
Soil	**Spirit**	**Soul**
Seed	**Thought**	**Mind**
Plant	**Manifestation**	**Body**

24. **Ts → I = L**
    Thoughts that lead to
    Identification equal
    Limitation

25. **J**   Just
    O   Over
    B   Broke

26. PI > N = FF

    Passive Income greater than necessities =
    Financial Freedom

27. P.I.P.R.E.

    Positive Income–Producing Real Estate

28. DP > DD

    Deposits greater than Deductions

29. H   Heading
    O   =   Off
    W   Wind

30. FFF—Financial Freedom Fund
    MPF—Major Purchases Fund
    EDU—Education Fund
    DON—Donation Fund
    FUN—Fun and Games Fund
    EXP—Expenses Fund

Daily Disciplines

SEVEN

MAGNETIZE YOUR GOOD

OK, now that we've finished the easy part, let's get to work!

I'm funnin' ya. You could start the book here. You could do both sections simultaneously. These next chapters are brief because you need to carry them in your pocket. These are the actions that, on a daily basis, catalyze your life so it must become what you have designed it to be.

Are you ready to receive your good?

Yes, or Yes?

If it came to you right now, would you stand up and take it, saying, "This is mine"?

Yes, or Yes?

I don't believe it.

If your boss walked up to you today and said, "You are doing a phenomenal job," or if your partner said, "Baby, you look terrific," or if your friend said, "You really give a lot," could you look each of them in the eye and say, "It's true, thank you"?

Probably not.

The very thought of uttering such *arrogant* words probably makes you cringe. You probably think you could never like anyone who would be so haughty as to accept the accolade as her due.

Well, wipe out Morocco on your list of possible vacation sites. Because in some parts of Morocco, it is the custom, when someone gives you a compliment, to say, as the only polite response: "It's true, thank you."

Hold out your hand and clench your fist. You can't receive anything like that, can you?

Chapters 1–6 were about preparing the vessel. They were about emptying out the old so you would have room for the new. Now you made the space for your good, but you can't receive it with a closed fist, a closed door, or a closed mind.

Do you like giving compliments and gifts? How does it make you feel when you tell someone how wonderful they are and they blush with pleasure? How do you feel when you give someone the perfect gift? How do you feel?

Damn good! This giving thing feels really good.

But have you ever told somebody they looked good or you liked their cooking or, for that matter, given any compliment, only to be told that you're wrong? Ever had somebody tell you why their offering was better last time, or it will be better next time, or you just don't know how bad whatever it is really was? How did you feel then?

I know I feel slimed. It's hard enough to muster the courage to give a robust compliment, but then to have it thrown back in your face: *yuk!*

And how many times a day do you do that, slime all over somebody's gift to you? If you're thinking, "Oh, I don't get many compliments," then I wonder—why not? Maybe you rejected so many that nobody bothers anymore.

We all know how good it feels to give a compliment, so why does it feel so bad to receive one?

I don't really want to know the answer to that, because it doesn't matter—anymore. From this day forward, you are going to graciously receive everything that comes your way. How are you going to do that?

With practice.

Perfect practice makes perfect. All the practices that follow, in this next section of the manual, are so simple to execute that you will execute them perfectly and, in no time, they will become the truth of your life. It works if you work it.

We all think of ourselves as such generous people. We love to give to others. It makes us feel so good. But what we don't see is how truly selfish we are, because the one thing most of us are an abomination at is giving others that same good feeling that we get from giving, by allowing ourselves to receive in a gracious manner.

Oh, I know the caution: "Pride goes before a fall." You don't want to be conceited.

You don't want to receive your good either.

One day I was having a barbecue and it started to rain. Well, I no longer allow rain on my parades, so I grabbed some tarps and clothespins and rope and proceeded to cover the deck. And I did a good job of it. The grill stayed dry, the tables and chairs stayed dry, the guests stayed as dry as they wanted to be. But after a while I noticed that the water was pooling along the outside of my deck. See, the rain that fell on the tarp was running off and pooling somewhere else.

And I had an *aha!*

If the rain is like our blessings and it pours down equally on all of us, good and bad alike, what happens if we block it?

It goes somewhere else.

Your blessings are trying to get to you, but if you don't want them, they're going to go to somebody else.

Francine's division was the most successful in her company. She knew that her twelve years of service and expertise had made it that way. While other departments lagged in profits and sales, Francine's made consistent steady gains quarter after quarter, reinventing itself and its market as technologies were invented or became obsolete.

The chief officers of Francine's firm came to her and offered her the position of managing officer of four other divisions. She perceived it as a lateral move. Although she would make more money and her responsibilities would be very different, she viewed it as a change that would cost her in time and stress as she struggled to bring the four other divisions up to the kind of productivity she had created in her own department. "Why should I give up being the superstar to become a new kid working up from the mailroom?" Every time they offered her the chance to move, Francine declined.

They eventually promoted a manager from one of the divisions that had been lagging behind to fill the position Francine had refused. Francine felt sorry for the guy who got the job and even felt for the company's officers, who hadn't been able to get a better man for the slot.

At the next quarterly meeting, Francine was shocked to see that those divisions had turned around. In her effort to stay the superstar on her own turf, Francine had not considered the fact that the principals had a clear and profit-motivated purpose in creating the new position. She told me, "They had modeled everything I had done in my department, and poured resources into the four departments, so they were now operating like a gigantic octopus, almost making my department obsolete." (Francine's company was using the 80:20 principle, which I will describe in the next chapter.)

Francine's division was eventually sold off, and she became part of the four-division conglomerate, where she continued to produce great profits and results, but that "gift" of something more had passed her by. She had allowed her present good to become the enemy of her better.

Have you ever done that?

Whatever you turn down, somebody else will take.

When you've offered or given something to someone and they rejected it, or didn't receive it graciously, did you ever want to return?

Probably not.

The parent of a friend of mine is an ambassador. As a result of her upbringing, her skills at saying "thank you" are so outstanding that after you've given her something and been so greatly appreciated, you can't wait to find another opportunity to give her something else. She knows how to receive.

If you don't know how to receive, somebody else will happily step up to take your place. So let's start with this prayer. Stand up, raise your arms overhead, outstretched to the sky, and say

> *"Universe, if there is anybody out there*
> *who has some good coming their way*
> *but they do not want it, send it to me.*
> *I am ready to receive."*

Do it again today and do it every day. Start your day in an attitude of receptive willingness to receive all the good that is constantly trying to get to you.

The next time someone gives you a compliment, take it. Say (aloud, preferably, but at least inwardly), "It's true, thank you." If you say the "It's true" part silently, then say the "thank you" out loud and with genuine pleasure. This response goes for sincere as well as insincere praise. Your part of this, not the other person's part, is yours to own and use.

Someone says, "You think you're hot shit?" Tell them, "It's true, thank you."

Someone says, "You're trying to outdo everybody!" Tell them, "It's true, thank you."

Someone says, "You're quite remarkable!" Tell them, "It's true, thank you."

You're a great cook, a wonderful friend, a fine performer, "It's true, thank you. It's true, thank you. It's true, thank you."

Cringe, roll over in your future grave, promise to kick yourself later, but now: Just say it. Because until you can say it without cringing, you will not be able to stand in agreement to accept your own good. And therein stands another aspect of the power of two or more. When you stand in agreement with another, you multiply the force and power of the thing desired. No matter that they may be speaking insincerely. The word has power. When you stand in agreement with words of power that are spoken for your good, you activate that good to speedily come your way.

It feels downright miserable to do this at first, but guess what? Current research in neuroscience has shown that if we change our behavior, we change our brain chemistry. New brain chemistry produces new thoughts. New thoughts generate new words that lead to new actions, new actions to new habits, new habits to new character, and new character to a new destiny.

So watch how you judge when other people stand in the power of their own glory, and know that you get what you give. But as you die to your idea of how anything should be, you receive the gift of making it possible for the very thing you once judged to now become your blessing.

If you haven't yet done the work in the first six chapters, do it now. Create the space to receive your good. Make a sign to the universe that you are ready.

Signs precede; they do not follow.

When Noah's ark had been at sea for forty days and forty nights, Noah sent the dove in search of land. At first the dove came back with nothing, but on the next trip it brought back the olive leaf. The olive leaf was the sign that dry land was near.

Form follows consciousness. If you develop the consciousness first, the form will manifest itself in your life. Noah didn't wait until he saw land. He sent the bird out because his consciousness had created the space for land.

You don't get the promotion first and then get to show the company how valuable you are.

Brad had a fair-to-middling business servicing computers. His biggest problem was that, because of the time it took to go from one client to another, he could spend more hours traveling than working and he never seemed to get ahead. Brad believed that he got all his work by providing quality service at a low price. He loved what he did, but he couldn't get ahead financially and he couldn't find time for his much-loved hobby of fixing up and reselling old cars.

I asked Brad if could see any way to increase his income and yet shorten his hours. He had thought it through and was absolutely certain there was no way. I then asked if he could imagine what his life would look like if he did earn more money and put in less time. He looked over his client list and told me it was nearly impossible, but agreed to pretend, which was a great start. "Fake it till you make it," I always say. I had Brad write down what his day would look like with more income and more free time. Then I asked him to start each ordinary day by reading through his written description of his ideal day, and to walk through his day with the energy that evoked in him, even as he was stuck in traffic, worrying about being late for all his computer appointments, or rushing through lunch. I gave him the method: "Hold the vision of that fabulous day, no matter how the day actually looks."

Brad told me that a reward came the first morning he used this method. A client offered to pay him his hourly rate for his travel to and from the company. This gave Brad the idea that he should ask for travel time fees from his other clients, but he was afraid of losing them and hesitated. I suggested he continue holding the vision of his life as he wanted it to be: with fewer hours and more earnings.

At the end of the first week Brad got a call from a company that wanted him to work exclusively for them, managing and serving their multimillion-dollar computer system. The job provided a healthy salary and good benefits and didn't require a regular eight-hour day. They needed him to be on call and available whenever a situation arose so they were willing to pay a premium.

Brad could hardly believe it. After one week of holding the consciousness of a life with less work and more money, it had materialized. He had not ever considered such a deal a possibility, so he hadn't sought it out. It had come knocking on his door.

Form follows consciousness.

When you can hold the vision of what you desire, no matter what the appearance of your life is, that vision must materialize.

The principle applies for bringing anything into your life that you desire. When you shift your consciousness, you create space for something new to present itself. You do not have to work for and earn your good, because when you can hold a relaxed state of consciousness that knows that good is always available, it will deliver itself to you.

If you find it hard to create the space in your mind, as a first practice, create it in your world.

You want some new furniture? Give away the furniture you already have to make space for it. You want a new partner? Make space for the new one by saying farewell to the partner you have. Don't wait until somebody new shows up, because who's going to show up in that situation? Who wants to accept part of a partner—since you haven't made an opening for a whole partner, have you?

Miranda was frustrated that she seemed to always be the one to make the plans for her friends to get together. She felt resentful and unappreciated. She complained, "No one ever calls *me* to make a date." I asked how often she called them. She said she thought being a friend meant it was important to call everyone at least once a week, and to see them once a month. I asked how that was working for her. Not very well. Her phone calls often went unreturned and she only managed to catch up with some friends a few times a year. "What would happen if you stopped calling?" I asked. I could see the panic rising in her flushed cheeks. "They would get mad at me! They might feel hurt, or think I didn't care about them."

"You mean they might feel just like you feel right now?" I asked.

"Yes." In that moment Miranda realized that all her calling and planning was not to make her friends feel better, but to keep herself from feeling bad. "I'm doing to them what I want them to do to me," she concluded. But she wasn't giving them a chance. I asked if she would write down what it would feel like to have fulfilling friendships. Then I asked her to start her day holding the consciousness that it was already done.

Her action task was to stop calling and making dates with anyone. Miranda told me the first week was very lonely. But on the weekend, one friend called wondering why he hadn't heard from her. During the next week Miranda began picking up some hobbies that she hadn't had time for, with her busy schedule maintaining her friendships. Then on an outing for supplies, she made a new friend. "We have so much in common; we both love knitting and sometimes we just drop by each other's house to share a new pattern or a new stitch. None of my other friends even knows how to knit." The new friendship was a great success. "I don't know who calls the other more," she said with a glowing smile.

As long as Miranda worked at having friendships, and filled up her time trying to maintain them, they evaded her. As soon as she decided what friendship would feel like to her, and then made the space for it to happen, it came knocking on her door.

What have you been putting effort into without getting results?

Shift your attention to what it is like to have what you desire. Don't worry about when, where, why, or how. Know that it is inevitable. All that we are and all that we do returns to us.

You want a life that you can be grateful for and excited about? Be grateful and excited about life! Signs precede; they do not follow. Your consciousness is the sign. When you cultivate a consciousness of love first, the outward form of love will show up in response to it. When you cultivate a consciousness of gratitude, a form of something to be grateful for will show up for you. When you form a consciousness of wealth now, the form of wealth must follow.

When you speak "It's true, thank you," to all expressions of your good, you are creating the sign, the consciousness, out of which all form ensues. From that, your good will materialize in the space you have prepared.

Sister Morningstar once told me that this moment was created in the past, but how we meet this moment creates our future. So when you can meet the moment in front of you—especially when it looks like limitation, lack, loss, and devastation—with an attitude of gratitude, what do you think you are creating for tomorrow?

More moments to be grateful for.

But if you greet it with denial, despair, disgust, and fear, what are you creating for tomorrow?

More moments to be disgusted with, despairing of, and afraid of. It's not supernatural magic, it's natural law. Your life will follow universal laws just as electricity and gravity follow their laws. Impersonal laws that work the same for everyone will not fail to work for you.

If you're meeting these words with skepticism, you're creating a future of skepticism.

What have you got to lose? You already know how to get it wrong. Many myths and legends put the power, the answer, the curve in the least likely of places: the hands of the fool or the eyes of a child. Carl Jung observed that of the four personality functions (feeling, thinking, sensing, and intuiting), an educated person has one superior function. The other part of the psychology that creates one's individual temperament is an equally opposing inferior function. Now we're going back to the fisher king fairy tale, to see how it works out. Our superior function leads us to our "fisher king" wound—remember, he was trying to seize the Holy Grail when he was hurt. But here's the ending: One day when the king is at his lowest ebb, a fool wanders into his castle. Being a fool, he doesn't realize he is in the presence of a wounded king, and sees only a man suffering. He asks the simplest of questions and responds in the least learned fashion to the despair of the king, and in a moment the wound is healed.

You carry with you, in every moment, all the tools you need to transform your life. Whatever it is in yourself that is needed at this moment to get where you need to go in the next moment, take hold of it, use it, don't reject it or ignore it as undignified, inferior, or foolish. Don't regard the power of your own persona with skepticism or suspicion; even if you think it a fool, let it help you.

Get over yourself.

Get over your need to be right rather than rich, safe rather than free, realistic rather than fulfilled. Make yourself, so you will be self-made rather than a bad version of somebody else's idea of who you should be.

If you do, you'll have no one but yourself to thank, and if you don't, you'll have no one but yourself to blame. You're the only one in your universe.

This runs counter to everything anyone has every told you. But how many of the people who told you how to get what you want even had what they wanted? So why did you listen to them? Do you ask a plumber how to plant your garden? Do you ask an accountant how to treat your pet's injuries? Do you ask a heart surgeon for artistic guidance? Take advice from people who know, and you will know they know by how they live.

Gauge expertise not by degrees or brochures; gauge it by the demonstration of expertise you need. Ask a real estate mogul to tell you where to buy property. Ask a millionaire to tell you where to invest money. Or better yet, try it out and learn it for yourself. That's what da Vinci did. He wasn't interested in anyone else's answers to questions; he wanted to find his own answers.

Don't take my word about receiving your good. Try it. Remember that whatever blessing you are blocking, there are plenty of us who are just waiting to receive it.

I have done most of my training work with actors, not just because I am one, but also because they need it most. Actors are the world's most unsuccessful group of professionals. Out of every thousand actors, 999 do not make a living in their chosen profession. Having now worked with scores of them, this is what I have surmised: Not only are most actors blocking their blessings, but they are, as a collective, attempting to block other people's blessings as well. By collectively bargaining to limit other actors' compensation, they have managed to seriously limit the compensation of the collective body of actors.

You can receive only what you give. In fact, the brain does not even distinguish between the self and the other. So psychologically, when you give to another, the brain perceives it as a gift to self, and responds accordingly. When research scientists have done studies using prayer to help in healing medical patients, who do you think received the greatest benefit, the ones praying or the ones being prayed for?

There are benefits to both groups, but the greater benefit has always accrued to those who prayed. Whatever you are thinking, wishing, or praying for on behalf of someone else, it will boomerang back at you.

I'm using actors as my examples, but what I'm speaking about also applies in your profession, job, home or community. Theater actors are the lowest paid of all actors, and in their most recent negotiations, they were not even negotiating for how much more they would get; they were negotiating for how small a decrease they would accept!

I stand by my belief that we get exactly what we want. Actors want less. Why else would they have, as part of their contracts, something called a "favored nations clause"? (I can speak of this freely here, because I've aired it at union contract talks, and the actors stand by it.) The clause says that producers have to pay all actors the same. But follow me: The actors give, as their intention for supporting this clause, the suggestion that it will raise salaries for all actors. If one nation gets it, all nations will get the same.

Well, whoever heard of such a ridiculous thing? Is that how the United Nations works? Do all nations even have equal votes, much less equal shares of anything? No.

There is nothing so unequal as treating unequals equally. And though, at our core, we actors are all equal in our function and capacity in our jobs, there are obvious differences or "inequalities." You don't expect the delivery clerk and the manager to get paid the same salary, do you? Why, then, would actors want a clause in their contracts requiring all actors to receive the same money and identical terms?

The result is obvious. After 101 years as a union, actors find themselves negotiating to take less than they've gotten before!

This is a law in operation: What you give, you receive. Are actors receiving less because the "favored nations" principle has delivered on the promise to raise everyone's salary? The short answer is "no." The long answer is "no way!"

What has happened is that, in trying to block everyone from freely negotiating whatever the market will allow, by trying to block other people from getting their full blessings, a few well-intentioned people have blocked blessings for actors as a collective.

But watch this: The salaries and terms for stars are actually without limit. Is it because stars are deemed a different kind of actor, under certain contracts, sometimes?

There is no logical market-driven answer for this well-known phenomenon. Mostly, it's because you cannot utterly block the generosity of the universe, just as you cannot stop the rain. When you try, it pools somewhere else. In the case of actors, many do sign "favored nations" contracts, but they also sign "side letters" giving them heaps more money and every term above and beyond the limitations of the clause. These separate side contracts are not governed by the union rules and the union does not have the ability to prevent anyone from entering into them. So actors are bound to a contract that, in trying to limit everyone's good, only limits the good of the majority.

I am reminded of basketball player Michael Jordan. While almost all the other players were renegotiating their contracts midstream, some even refusing to perform, Jordan worked under a contract that was substantially less than the market would allow for his ability and skill. Jordan gave much more than he was given, and the universe responded by making him one of the most successful entertainment figures in history. He gave his best despite what he was being given, and it came back to him a million-fold.

Where are you doing this in your own life? Where are you giving less because you expect more? You get what you give. You want more love in your life? Give more love to others. Want more friendship and comfort? Go out and be more of a friend. Want more opportunities? Provide more opportunities for others.

Remember the story of that minister who went to speak at a new parish and put a $20 bill into the offering box? He got $20 because he gave $20, and he was content and happy with that $20, but his little boy pointed out that had he given more, he would have gotten more. If you had put in more, at some point in your past, would you have gotten more? That last failed job: How much more could you have put in? That failed marriage: How much more could you have put in?

You get what you give.

He who forgives most is most forgiven.

Although you can only get what you give, you do not get what you give if you're giving with the idea that you are priming the pump, in order to get. If you give with the expectation of reciprocity, what will you get? A gift that has its own string attached.

Unfortunately, most of our love relationships have become this way. We give because the person makes us feel so good; but when they don't make us feel good, for a day or for too many days, we stop giving. True giving expects no return. True giving is what I experienced from the man at my church. It is a reward to both the giver and the receiver, and so is magnified and multiplied by its free release.

Gratitude is the most powerful force in the universe. Gratitude is receptive. This is why they say we have one mouth for talking but two ears for listening. Gratitude is the eternal listening to the universe in its graceful givingness to each of us.

When you are truly grateful for all that you have, then and only then will you receive more to be grateful for. Gratitude creates the overflow.

Like attracts like, and whatever vibration you are sending into the universe will draw its like vibration, like a magnet, back to itself. You already know what you're sending out because you can look at what you're getting back.

Perfect practice makes perfect. So today, and every day, begin practicing.

First: Practice standing in agreement with your good, by saying, until it permeates your consciousness: "It's true, thank you," to any and all statements that reflect the good you are now choosing for yourself.

Second, find something to be grateful for in every moment. If you stop at the ATM machine and find the account low, be grateful you found out so you can add funds before checks start bouncing. If the car breaks down before your vacation, be grateful it happened now so you won't be stranded. If a lover leaves you, be grateful that space is being made for the right partner to come your way.

How are you going to cultivate this attitude of gratitude? The same way you found something to want for yourself.

Make Something Up.

The practice of cultivating gratitude is what we're after, and it stops the practice of complaining, which we'll tackle in Chapter Nine, the chapter about your word being law in the universe.

| SEVEN: PRACTICES |

FOR RECEPTIVITY: In the face of all *words* of praise, whether they are sincere or not: *"It's true, thank you,"* or simply, "Thank you, I appreciate that."

FOR ABUNDANCE: Whenever you see anything in abundance, be it a pile of dirt, a highway full of traffic, garbage piled on the street, whatever it is, say to yourself: *"I live in a world of abundance."*

FOR PEACE: In all circumstances, even in the midst of wars and rumors of wars, chaos on your job or conflict in your family, say: *"Peace is unfolding easily and effortlessly."*

FOR LOVE: In the face of human rejection or self-deprecation, know absolutely: *"The universe is loving me through everyone and every thing I meet."*

FOR RUNNING LATE: *"I am in divine time."*

FOR ANSWERS: During exams, interviews, auditions, in response to demands for solutions: *"I may not know the answer, but there is an answer, and it can flow through me."*

FOR SAFETY: In new situations or unknown environments: *"I am divinely guided, directed, and protected."*

FOR GRIEF: In times of loss or mourning: *"Sorrow may endure for a night, but joy comes in the morning."*

FOR STRENGTH: When the task at hand feels bigger than you are: *"Spirit, empty me of myself and fill me with you."*

FOR MATERIAL LOSS: *"Naked I came from my mother's womb and naked I will depart. The Spirit giveth, and Spirit has taken away. All praise to the Spirit."*

EIGHT

MAKE YOUR ENERGY MATTER

Everything in this manual works if you work it. Have you been working it?

Good.

Now we're ready to talk about making your energy matter.

If I can show you how to magnify your energy and multiply the results you get, would you be interested in that?

And if I can show you how to minimize or dissolve the situations that cause you the most grief, would you be interested in that?

Good.

Let me ask you this: Do you still save for a rainy day? Do you know what your energy is focused on creating?

More rainy days!

Do you still pay your debts first? You know what your energy is creating? More debts for you to pay!

Have you already started to pay yourself first? You know what your energy is creating? Getting paid more.

Pablo Picasso was one of the most prolific and wealthy artists in history. Unlike most artists, he experienced his fame, wealth, and success during his lifetime. Do you know what Picasso did that made him different from most of the other artists in history? Early in his career, Picasso made a decision: He was going to put his energy only into painting, and he was going to make a living solely by making his art. True, sometimes he lived well and sometimes he did not. But by the end of his life he had amassed enough private wealth to leave for generations after him.

How did he accomplish this? By directing his energy.

A → E → R

Where your Attention goes

→ **Energy flows**
→ **and Results show.**

Did you ever notice that as soon as you learn a new word or hear of a new product—*bam!*—suddenly it's everywhere? Do you think it just magically appeared as soon as you became aware of it? No, it's always been there but, because your attention was not on it, it didn't appear to you. It may as well not have existed, because it was invisible in your world.

Why is this meaningful for us? Because wherever your attention is, you have given that a lot of your energy, so it shows up in a big way in your life.

Why do we put our attention in one place instead of another? It's usually because we believe it's important or it's the only thing we know. So, for example, say you have a belief that being a good person means helping out when a friend or family member is in trouble. I'd wager most people have that belief; I know I always did.

The problem is: What is going to be genuinely helpful to somebody who is in trouble? Of course, the answer depends on the kind of trouble and the particular person, right? Or does it? I bet you don't just do the same thing for every person every time. You figure out what will be the most helpful. You put some thought and energy into how to help out. And for every ounce of the thought and energy you send someone else's way, there's a little bit left for your own stuff.

I know explosions are going off for some of you. Write it down.

_____

_____

_____

_____

_____

This false belief—which really amounts to thinking you know how to do someone else's living better than they can do it for themselves—robs you of the energy to make your own life better.

How many times a day do you offer advice? How many minutes of a day are you figuring out someone else's problem? What happens if you stop?

The first thing that happens is an end to a lot of conversation. It's awkward. Someone pours out his tragic story and you don't offer one iota of useful, helpful information. You simply listen, nod, and say, "I'm sorry about that." Or someone tells you how wrong or bad you are for not doing (or being, or giving them) what they want and you simply say, "I wish it was . . ." (whatever way they wanted it to be). The stories don't have to be sad either. Maybe there's a great story somebody else has that can divert and activate you into joining their next quest. How many times have you found yourself helping other people fulfill their dreams, while yours lie wasting?

But . . . but . . . that's what good people do.

Good people do all sorts of things.

You can keep on doing whatever you have already been doing if you choose, but if you ever want to create something big for yourself, the first step is doing what is yours to do and allowing others to do the same.

What *is* yours to do?

If you have children, a husband, lover, friend, boss, coworker, what is yours to do? You love them, feed them, clothe them, educate them, and encourage them. But it is not yours to do, for instance: to fight their battles; to make their decisions; or to arrange their futures. If you have a friend in need, it's yours to listen if asked, to love, even to criticize if, and only if, you have asked permission and it has been granted. (It took me years to get this one, because I am a born crusader. The blood of Joan of Arc runs through my veins. Give me a cause, show me an underdog, and I am on the case. At a silent meditation retreat bringing in the year 2005, I realized that what I had been doing with my life up to that moment was demonstrating the Crucifixion and the Resurrection again and again. It hit me that Christ did it only once. So maybe it wasn't mine to keep doing.)

What is yours to do? It's the most important question there is, but you've probably never asked it. Because most of us have been acculturated to the idea, and the habit, of just doing whatever needs to be done—or whatever appears to need to be done—next. We rarely ask if we can even do it well; we simply jump in and do what's expected or asked of us. If there's a problem, we hasten to fix it—even though, at times, we inadvertently make it worse.

I'd like to introduce you to the Pareto Principle, formulated by Dr. Joseph Juran, based on the economic principles and observations of Vilfredo Pareto. Pareto was a nineteenth-century economist and farmer who observed that 20 percent of his crops produced 80 percent of his harvest. Dr. Juran furthered the investigation of this phenomenon and discovered that it applied in virtually every economic situation. It is now known as the 80:20 principle. Understood and used along with the technique of consciously directing your energy, this principle can help you decide where to direct your energy.

The 80:20 principle says, for instance:

- You wear 20 percent of your clothes 80 percent of the time.
- 20 percent of the items on your "To Do" list get you 80 percent of the value you desire, while 80 percent of your challenges come from 20 percent of what you consider to be your issues or concerns.

- In sales, 20 percent of the sales force produces 80 percent of the revenues.
- In meetings, 80 percent of decisions come from 20 percent of the meeting time.

Imagine if we could determine in advance the 20 percent of our efforts that would produce 80 percent of our rewards: All our lives would be instantly transformed!

That's what we are going to do. You're going to do it because this is an area where you can't take anybody else's example or advice. What is meaningful or rewarding to you may be a challenge or chore to somebody else. So let's make a "To Do" list. What are the top ten things you need to accomplish in the next week? Write it down.

This week, as you set out checking off the items you have accomplished and crossing them off the list, I'm going to ask you to keep a separate journal of all the secondary gains and peripheral benefits that come from the completion of each task. It could be simple things: Maybe you slept longer and were able to get something else accomplished because you were rested, or you had time to create because you were no longer stalling and worrying about completing a task. The benefits will go on long past the week. So you are to keep writing the benefits beyond this week. Because this is how you are going to know what percent of your energy gets you the most rewards.

No person will complain of the want of time who never loses any.
—Thomas Jefferson

If only 20 percent of our effort produces 80 percent of our results, what about the other 80 percent of our effort? Well, if we are not consciously directing our energy, that 80 percent of our efforts is not only *not* producing the rewards we desire, but 20 percent of that effort is giving us 80 percent of the things we definitely want less of. And if this is an economic principle or law, how do we fight it?

We don't fight it.

We use it and flow with it to get us exactly where we want to go. You see businesses using the 80:20 principle every day with something as simple as "loss leaders." A loss leader is a product that is advertised and priced so low the retailer is practically giving it away. Why? Because the retailer knows that the advertised low price of that sought-after product will get you into the store, and while you're in that store, you'll buy other products that you hadn't even been thinking about purchasing.

You can put the 80:20 principle into practice in the simplest way at home. Notice what clothes you wear the most. Have a favorite outfit you've been wearing to death? From now on, buy more versions of that outfit and cut back on all the extraneous, random, odd items that serve you on far fewer occasions. You will be dressing better soon and saving money as well.

Pat had an in-home business buying and reselling merchandise on the Internet. The problem, he told me, was that he didn't know what people would buy until they bought it, so he had a constant supply of stuff filling his house and garage and making life almost unlivable for his family. There was nowhere to move around. He'd been in business for ten years and made lots of money, enough to buy a nice new house, but he'd also collected a lot of junk that was filling it up.

I asked if he'd kept a record of his sales. "Somewhere in these stacks," he answered. I suggested that he hire his kids to find those records, and go through and sort them by the kind of item sold and the amount of profit made on each. It took a couple of months for them to complete that task. But a pattern emerged immediately. First, Pat pinpointed which items turned the greatest profit, and by the end he learned which items sold the greatest volume. He also discovered the turnaround time for purchases and sales and seasonal patterns for specific items. Now he could implement a plan for maximizing sales and minimizing the space his merchandise took up.

Armed with the information hidden in his own records, Pat was able to clean out his house. He then put his kids to work finding more of the items that sold the most and brought in the best profits. They were delighted with their new responsibilities and eager to outdo each other in their jobs. The 80:20 principle helped Pat turn a thriving business that had increased his wealth but cramped his lifestyle into a family endeavor that multiplied in benefits far beyond the number on the bottom line.

"The vital few and the trivial many." You devote your attention to the vital few so as not to be besieged by the trivial many.

As we are creating a life unlike anyone has ever lived, we focus our energy so that it is producing maximum results. So the first question in determining what is yours to do is to ask: Could someone else do this job?

Don't distract yourself with rationalizations. There are endless reasons for you to run yourself ragged doing every trivial thing yourself. None of those reasons holds water. Think it's easier and less of a headache for you to just do things yourself, rather than to delegate? Not if you set things up properly. You simply need to figure out what tasks could be done by someone else. You see, all your reasonable, rational justifications and excuses have tied up your energy on trivial tasks that gain you meager results.

Give them up. Could someone else do this job?

Take something as simple as laundry. For most of us, the job takes a couple of hours a week. If you have a large family, it can take an entire afternoon. Could somebody else do it? Oh sure, you get other things done while you're doing it. Could somebody else do it? The short answer is yes; the longer answer is, "you bet!" For $20 a week, somebody else can probably do your laundry. Then you'll have two hours of open time to concentrate your energy on something that only you can do, something from the "vital few."

What about the business you wanted to start, the book you're going to write, the invention that's been spinning around for years in your mind, the painting? So many things you say you want to do, but you just can't find the time.

I just found you two hours a week. That's 104 hours a year—four whole twenty-four-hour days—to get more than started on whatever you really want to do with your life.

There are so many tasks in our life that somebody else could do—and do better than we do. Letting them do it frees you up to do what only you can do, to do what no one else but you can do.

Who else can draw that particular painting you see in your mind's eye?

Who else can design that system that you've been tinkering with in the garage?

Who can overhaul that marketing plan?

Who can start that business that has never existed?

You can—if you begin looking at the things you do that someone else can do for you, so that you can do what no one else can do for you.

The garden: For some people it's a gift and an art; for others it's a joyless chore. If you're in the latter group, let someone else do it. Grocery shopping, cooking, fact checking, there are myriad tasks that, if you allowed someone else to do for you, you'd have plenty of time and energy to do what you want.

And if you're still thinking, "I can't afford that," then you probably haven't begun using the financial freedom system from Chapter 6. And if you've started and are still waiting for the wealth to pour in, then let some of those trivial tasks go undone for a while so your energy can create the wealth that will get them taken care of by somebody else.

I am a single mother raising two children full-time and two teenagers part-time. I am a Tony Award–winning actress, lecturer, trainer, author, painter, singer, and composer. I couldn't do it without help. But I know that no one else can get on the stage for me, stand in front of the cameras for me, or sing the songs for me. For me, then, my job is clear. Anything that interferes with that is not mine to do. No one else can kiss my babies' owwies or tell them I love them, but someone else can make their lunch or set out tomorrow's clothes in the morning.

Time and energy are your most valuable resources; you need to conserve and wisely use your resources. Reclaim what you are throwing away. Begin by looking at where your time and energy are going.

If you're sitting down paying bills as they come in, when are you creating the business that's going to pay them for you? Set aside one time in the month to pay bills, and spend the rest of that time thinking up wealth-generating ideas.

I am an actress, but I've also envisioned myself as a businesswoman. In the beginning, I had my hands in everything. I did my own press packets, checked out who was creating new projects, researched every aspect of the business I was starting, made all the phone calls for that personal touch, arranged my own meetings, took every phone call—on and on. I was my business; there was just me. But as my ideas began to take real form, it was too much for one person; I couldn't do it all. You want to grow to the place where you can't do it all. You want to grow to the place where it takes a great team to carry out all the aspects of the visions and dreams you have called forth.

Do you think Oprah Winfrey can do all the tasks of running her show, her magazine, or TV channel, plus the film projects, book clubs, and so on? Can Bill Gates oversee every new Microsoft product from conception through creation, manufacture, testing, marketing, and distribution? How could he even be in all those places at the same time? Imagine Oprah saying, "I can't do the show today because I've got to read all the books that are going to be considered for the book club." Do you actually think any successful business operates that way: with one person doing everything? But it's how we run our lives, trying to do it all, and all by ourselves.

As stated earlier, Archimedes discovered the principle of the lever. By using the same amount of force, using a lever, you can have a greater effect. Only by leverage can you geometrically increase the results you gain in every aspect of your life and business. But how do you increase leverage?

You increase leverage by asking for, and allowing yourself to receive, the benefit of other people's time, energy, and money. You increase leverage by creating a team. To use Mark Victor Hansen's acronym:

> *Together*
> *Everyone*
> *Achieves*
> *More*

Your team might be your family. You can all work together to achieve what you all desire. Family restaurants operate this way, and they're a pleasure to watch. For a business, your team should ideally be your coworkers. The point is to create a team. There are specific ways of doing that. Because the team is only as effective as its members, each member must be doing what she does best and must also be doing, within the team, what only she can do.

If your thoughts, which are your energy, are going toward building a team and creating the wealth to accomplish your goal of delegating the many trivial tasks essential to everyday living, what are you creating? A life where you are doing what you love, and you can afford to have everything that supports your life taken care of for you by others.

My accountant Derek Folk says, "If you want to be a billionaire, you have to create a lot of millionaires." Your wealth will create wealth for others. The efforts you put into building your dreams create opportunities for others to fulfill their own dreams. When you create more wealth for yourself, you are creating more wealth for others and giving to the universe, and it all comes back to you.

> A hundred times every day I remind myself that my inner and
> outer life depend upon the labors of other men, living and dead,
> and that I must exert myself in order to give in the measure as I
> have received and am still receiving.
>
> —Albert Einstein

Attention → Energy → Results

In its most basic form, where is your attention right now? The attention you place on others affects them too. So if your energy is on solving their problems, what are you helping them create? More problems for you to solve.

But if your attention is on how much faith and trust you have that they can work things out for themselves, what are you helping them create? More opportunities to work things out for themselves.

> The greatest discovery of my generation is that a human being
> can alter his life by altering his attitudes.
>
> —William James

Not only our thinking, but our behaviors, are influenced by the thinking and the behaviors of those around us. Ken Keyes, Jr., wrote about a phenomenon observed in 1952 on the island of Koshima, Japan. There is a colony of Macaca fuscata monkeys living on the island. They were all given sweet potatoes dipped in sand. The monkeys loved the taste of sweet potatoes but disliked the sand. One day, a monkey named Imo began to wash her potatoes. She taught this to her immediate family and gradually, between 1952 and 1958, all the monkeys on the island took up the practice of washing the sand off their sweet potatoes.

One day it was observed that the practice had miraculously jumped across the sea. The monkeys on the island of Takasakiyama, as well as monkeys living on the mainland, also began to wash their sweet potatoes.

This has been called the hundredth monkey phenomenon, though the exact number of monkeys who were washing their potatoes when the behavior transferred to the unconnected monkey colonies is not known. What is important for us to glean is that our thoughts are not only producing results for ourselves, but for our children, our families, our coworkers, our friends—even our enemies.

There can be no selfishness in this practice, for what we do to and for ourselves, we do to and for others; what we do to others, we do to ourselves. We cannot want success at the expense of another's failure without drawing failure upon ourselves. Sadly, we can wish all the joy, love, and success imaginable on others, but they still may choose to block it or refuse to receive it. What we cannot do is to wish upon others any fate without calling it down upon ourselves, at some point in time, in some fashion.

So how many thoughts did you have today about how so-and-so cannot function without you? Are you willing to change that thought to: "So-and-so can accomplish everything he desires without any assistance from me"? So what if you don't believe it: Think the thought. Put some energy on that: somebody else's happiness, success, joy, fulfillment. By genuinely doing so, you are creating it for yourself.

Albert Einstein said that energy cannot be created or destroyed. What does that mean for you and me, who simply desire more freedom and energy in our everyday lives? It is both simpler and harder than we thought. We can do it—give ourselves more energy—any time we choose. We hold the ultimate responsibility. And there is no one to blame if we don't go for it, and in fact, get it, for it's ready for us when we are ready.

Do you want more time and energy for the things you love?

Put more time and energy into them. Take some part of every day to do just one task. Visualize one picture of what you are making of your life right now.

It's all now. It's not how-it's-gonna-be, or how you want it to be. Put time and energy into seeing it as it is now. Let the now of your dreams be the only reality you give your energy to, and it will become the now of your reality.

If you don't have what you want and you're not where you want to be, don't fight it. Your past thoughts created this moment. Just create a new tomorrow by taking this moment to give all your energy to the joy and success and love and gratitude that you have in the world: You are creating that world with this very thought.

If you don't have what you want, you can't help anybody else get what they want, can you?

I know you've got a list of people you helped get where they are, and sure, they've thanked you for all your help. The truth is: Their commitment to receiving and having your help is what got it for them in the first place. The energy they put into saying "yes" is what brought you to their assistance. No amount of energy you put toward someone who doesn't really want success, or isn't ready to receive their blessings, is going to get them anything—and that includes yourself.

So if it isn't here, or on its way, look at where you are putting your energy. This holds true for the things we want out of our life as well. First of all, we don't have to change the world or the people around us or even our circumstances to change our thinking. But when we change where we put our energy, the circumstances and people around us will either change or we will continue to build our dreams in the midst of the old chaos, and it will have no effect on us.

What do I mean by saying you can succeed in the middle of the unchanged world around you? Remember Meshach, Shadrach, and Abednego from the Bible story in the Book of Daniel? There they were, in the midst of the fiery furnace, but they were not singed. You don't have to be rescued out of the fire; you can be saved right in the middle of it. The hot flames can be disintegrating everything around you, but you can stand there, not only untouched but elevated and magnified because of your ability to withstand it.

After the meditation retreat, I decided that I wanted no more Crucifixions and Resurrections. Instead, I was going to be a demonstration of the givingness, ease, and grace of the universe. But, I thought, there's all this press I get about the hardships I've endured. What about that? I decided I would not give it any more energy by not talking about it again. I decided to rewrite my story to exclude divorce and legal custody battles. I stopped talking about them.

You know what happened?

They disappeared from my life.

At my next interview, the reporter, instead of asking about the "bad times," asked, "Are you talking about that?" I said, simply, "No, I'm not."

Then the plot of *All My Children* developed the biggest custody case in the history of the show, going between *All My Children* and *One Life to Live*, the Chandlers versus the Buchanans, and I was one of the attorneys. I was doing *Caroline, or Change* at the time, though, so they shot the scenes without you ever seeing the attorneys. I wasn't talking about these things in life, in interviews, on the stage, or on TV! I was free.

Meanwhile, a huge piece of the thirteen-year legal battle in my life was also scheduled for a hearing and a trial. I arrived at court in New York only to discover that the time of the hearing was incorrect. I was there in the morning; the trial was in the afternoon, but I had a massage and lots of nice things planned for my afternoon. So I put to the test this work I'm calling on you to do now. I was not compelled to be in court; I was not under subpoena. I was there because it was my trial, but it was also my choice. I asked myself, "Do I want to spend my day in 'trial' or in 'pampering'?" I chose pampering, excused my own absence from the trial, and went about my real business.

You know what happened?

The lawyers walked into court and the judge said there was not going to be a trial. And there was none. My attorney prevailed in a yearlong motion on her paperwork alone.

Had I energized the situation with my presence, who knows how long it would have continued. It had been sucking up my energy for thirteen years. In that moment when I removed my energy from it, it fell.

| EIGHT: PRACTICES |

Attention → Energy → Results

Where attention goes, energy flows and results show.

Sometimes it's easier to know what we don't want rather than to know what we do want. If there is something you know you want to remove from your life, be it an illness, a nasty relationship, poverty, loneliness, whatever your "fiery furnace" is that you feel locked inside, start by *never speaking about it again.* We will delve deep into this practice in the next chapter. For now, remember: Speech is energy. Don't give the negative aspects of your life any of your energy. Starve them *out*!

When you want to remove something from your life,

> *Remove your attention from it.*
> *Think about what you do want.*
> *Talk about what you do want.*
> *Go where you want to be.*
> *Walk around as if it is gone.*

And it will be.

When you want to create something, anything, in your life,

> *Think about it.*
> *Talk about it.*

Tell somebody else about it.
Spend time where it is,
and with the people who have it.
Wish it for somebody else.
Walk around as if it already is.
Hold space for it in the silence.

And watch it all fall into place.

Here are the applications:

For Health: Do not speak that you are ill.

When there is pain in one part of the body,
focus your words and attention
on a different part of the body
that is functioning perfectly and feeling great.

To contain and reserve personal energy and power:

Ask permission before offering opinions, help, or advice.
Respect when you are told no thank you.
Always see others as doing their lives perfectly.

The attention and energy you send out always returns to you. Be sure you are always giving what you want to see coming back to you in return.

NINE

MAKE YOUR WORD
LAW IN THE UNIVERSE

Let's begin with a powerful affirmation. Put your hand over your heart and say:

I give up my good girl/boy act
today and forever.

Are you ready to trade in being a good boy for being a powerful boy?

Are you ready to trade in being a good girl for being a strong and incredibly fulfilled girl?

Prove it. Answer this question. How are you doing?

_____

_____

_____

If what you wrote is anything less than what you will say the moment after all you desire is fulfilled, then it is blocking that desire from being fulfilled. From this moment on, you are going to begin living and speaking from the moment after your dreams are fulfilled.

Your "I am" statements call that world into being.

I am. It's the shortest sentence in the language. By your word in the form of "I am" statements, you call everything in your world into being, and you die to an infinite number of alternate possibilities. So if I ask again: How are you? What do you have to say?

_____

_____

_____

Maybe you still don't know what to say, or you think there is some "right" answer, or you just feel bad right now. It's the perfect place to begin because, whether you believe it or not, your word is law in the universe. Everything you speak comes to pass.

So why don't you have what you want? You say you did call forth that job promotion? Well, maybe you called it forth on a Tuesday, but that Friday you told somebody what a headache those new responsibilities would be. Maybe you called it forth by one word and sent it back by the next. Could it be that you do this about everything, all day long, every day, year in and year out?

Your word is one of the most powerful tools for creating the life you want, for being the person you dream of being. So when you say "I am . . . ," you no longer want to speak about the temporary stages that just mark the path as you unfold to your greater being. You want to speak from the eternal sense of your being. You want to speak what is true and unchanging about yourself in every moment.

When you are asked how you are doing, you want to say words like:

I am outstanding.

I am perfect, whole, and complete.

I am divine.

I am blessed.

I am unfolding perfectly.

It sounds hokey, doesn't it? Most of the time you don't *feel* that way. But until you begin to speak it, you won't feel that way.

Part of our good girl/boy act is the belief that we must tell "the truth." But whose truth are we telling? Say you're walking around coughing and sneezing and someone asks, "Are you sick?" In that moment your nose is running and your head is about to explode, yet you have the opportunity to either focus on your discomfort or to call forth your healthy reality. You get to choose. You can stand in agreement with their description of your world, and even magnify your experience of that miserable reality by saying "yes," and then giving the litany of symptoms, or you can choose different and say, "No, in fact health and vitality are coursing through me." (Of course, health and vitality are in fact coursing through you; that's how you are going to recover from the temporary effects of that soon-to-be-ignored-away rhinovirus!)

It's not a lie. It's a choice, to focus your attention and give your energy to the greater truth that you want to constantly reflect your life. When your nose is stuffy or when any part of your body is in pain, it's only a part. There are many other parts of your body where health and vitality are flowing fully and freely, and even rallying the resources you need. Put your attention there. Then that energy will grow and spread to cover your entire being. In the alternative, you magnify the energy of illness so that it grows and spreads, and soon a silly little cold has you utterly weakened, laid out in the bed.

This is no joke. You speak your health and not your disease. So what if the person who asked the question is looking at you like you're crazy, or fleeing lest she catch not only your cold but what she perceives as the *mental illness* that has you denying "reality." Do you really care what she thinks of you? She's directing her attention to your cold; you don't have to do the same, do you?

Say something appears to go wrong and someone asks, "Are you okay, can I help?" OK, maybe you're in a puddle on the floor, but you speak: "I'm great, fantastic. I can handle it. Thank you for asking." Some people will think you're crazy, you're in denial, but just as many people may think, "Wow, what positive attitude! You don't let anything get you down." Which is more important to you? You get to choose. You can choose to intensify and energize the very things you don't want in your life, or you can choose to energize and reflect what you do want in your life. When you say, "I can handle it," you can.

What's the point of saying something that's just not true, and everybody knows it, and everybody can see it? Isn't that living in denial?

Hey, you get to choose. You can stand in agreement with most people in the world, who live in personal environments of lack, loss, limitation, disease, discomfort, and discouragement because that's what they see in the world and that's what they speak of the world. On the other hand, you can be in the world but not of it.

This is about taking ultimate responsibility and accountability for all that you are. It has been said that power is the time between thinking or speaking about something and its actually happening. The work in this manual increases your power and decreases the time between thought, word, and manifestation.

You begin to take responsibility for your word by saying what you mean, doing what you say.

"But, but—a lot of times I don't think before I speak."

Right. Do you want to keep doing that?

"But that's so much work, choosing your words so carefully."

Right. Your unconscious, unthinking, careless choices got you where you are today. Do you want to stay there?

"I'm not going to lie and say things that just aren't true."

Right. You can keep your life just the way it is, which is to say, you can keep your life the way you see it now. But the life you are creating as you do this work is the real truth, so which lie would you choose: a lie of disease, distress, discomfort, and discouragement, or a lie of joy, happiness, fulfillment, and success? It is your choice.

This moment of experience, right now, was created by your thoughts, words, and actions in the past. It has no power; it is already done, and will pass quickly if you allow it. Its only hope to continue is by your giving it energy right now. Your attention and words give it the power to linger in your life; power it would not have if you simply turned your attention away from it.

It's not always easy, but we're not looking for perfection. Once you accept the idea that you called forth whatever is in your life, there is no one to blame and no need to prolong the agony of the status quo.

Once, several years ago, after I had gotten off welfare, I was working as a substitute schoolteacher and doing various odd jobs, but my paychecks weren't getting to me. For about six months, every payment that was due to me failed to come through on time, if at all. One day I asked myself, "Why do I believe I should work and not get paid for it?"

And you know what came up from inside me? I remembered a series of incidents when I had complained: "Whenever I work, so-and-so takes all my money!"

Is that clear to you? Because it was clear to me. By my words, I had called forth the reality that when I worked, my money would be taken away, and the universe had fulfilled my order. But now that I was aware of it, I could—and did—change my words to "My wealth is unfolding right now," and pretty soon it was.

This moment was created by what you said in your yesterdays, but what you say today calls forth your tomorrows.

There are myriad situations in which this comes up. In the beginning, you need to write the script. When someone calls attention to something you are consciously removing your attention from, what are you going to say? Whatever it is must be a reflection of the life you want. Let's try out some say-sos.

"Man, I'm so sorry about that car accident. That's gonna be a big headache." You might say, "It's gonna be a blessing or a gift to me. I'm insured and I'm claiming it." And they say with that tone of the skeptic: "Oh sure, sure," and you answer, "It's true, thank you."

Someone says: "You look terrible, maybe you should go home." And you reply, "I feel fabulous—do you need to go home?" Give people's negativity back to them if you want, but never let them focus their negativity on you.

As you begin to write these scripts, you will notice that only certain people try to project negative perspectives on you. Maybe you'll want to re-think your relationships with those people. Of course, some of these folks may be in your immediate family or your workplace and you can't just get away from them. But you can choose not to accept their contagion.

Magazines and newspapers have often written about the difficult challenges I have faced. I don't deny them, but I can speak to the gifts they have given me, and thereby I practice naming and claiming blessings from everything in my life.

What is the good you desire?

Name it and claim it.

And only speak of it as if it's done. That house is mine. That car is mine. That job is mine. In *Learned Optimism,* author and psychologist Martin Seligman says that optimistic people have a less realistic view of the world than pessimistic people, who see the world more accurately. But optimistic people, because of their positive view, tend to create what they want despite the "realistic" obstacles that keep the more accurate, pessimistic people stalled. Is it accuracy you're after, or a good life? The research says you get to choose!

Cultivate relationships with optimistic people. If you tell a friend your good news one day, and he reminds you that once, long ago, you told him that you were hoping for that, he's a supportive and energetic optimist. He remembered your dream all along. Be grateful and tell him so; also tell him more of your hopes and ambitions, for he was standing in agreement with you when you made your wish in the past. He expected you to succeed, and you did. He wasn't expecting you to fail or waiting to say, "I told you so," if you stumbled. By the same token, avoid people who load you down with discouragement. There is plenty of disappointment in the world; you don't need reminders of that.

You want to create a life that is immune to the passing realities of the stock market, crime, and politics? You can be in the world, but not of it; you can live the life you dream of, no matter what everybody else's life looks like. Maybe you'll even inspire someone to follow in your footsteps.

So as you gain in your experience and the practice of making your word law in the universe, you must also:

Honor all your commitments.

Not just commitments to others, but commitments to yourself. This means if you tell someone you will do something or be somewhere, and as life happens, you need to change things, you must first get their permission.

Yeah, it sounds awful. You promised your kid you'd go to the game and now you have an opportunity to meet a prospective business client. Which is more important: that your word be law, or that you continue calling things forth only to send them back, calling them forth and sending them back? Then you never get out of the limbo land, because you have not been clear about what you are calling forth.

When you are asking someone's permission to break your word, you must be sincere. You cannot do this right if you have already decided that you're doing what you want, no matter what. So when you ask, you don't start with: "Look, I've got this . . ." You start with: "I said that I would . . . Is there any possibility that we could reschedule it to another time?" And you wait for the answer. And you listen for what they want or expect of you. From the place of considering their needs as well as your own, you decide whether it is of the utmost importance to honor your first commitment. You can break that first commitment if and only if it will be acceptable to the person to whom that commitment was made.

This is about responsibility and accountability. If you blow off your first commitment, you are creating the possibility, even the probability, of getting blown off in your own future. This may even come from the person with whom you are trying to rearrange commitments. Remember: How you do anything is how you do everything. Honor your commitments so that you create honor for commitments to yourself in the future.

The same goes, naturally, for commitments to self. If you make a commitment to yourself and decide you want to change it, you need to speak to yourself, thus: "I formally de-commit from . . ." Whatever it is, be it going to the gym, or making a call, or taking a class; anything you have committed to do for yourself, honor it or get your own conscious permission to change it.

There are many times when our words do just spill forth in anger or reaction. Sometimes our self-talk can be filled with negativity, when we are sad or hurting. How can we deal with this?

This next exercise was given to me by Reverend Michael Beckwith. It is an exercise for taking the power of intense emotion and using it to call forth your good. Say you are stuck in traffic and late for an important meeting. Your first tendency would be to curse the traffic, the other drivers, and blame yourself. Maybe you don't talk aloud to yourself, but you sit in your car fuming or crying. Instead, speak out, and instead of cursing the world, with all the force of your rage, pain, and hurt, speak the positive things you desire: "I am the luckiest person in the world, things always go perfectly for me, my timing is always perfect, I am never late, everything goes exactly my way." You are taking the powerful energy of emotion and, instead of letting it be a wildfire raging over all your good works and intentions, you are directing it to bringing forth more and greater good. And at the very least, you'll have yourself cracking up with laughter in a few minutes.

Traffic, lovers, money, life: We must in every moment make the effort to give our attention, in thought, word, and speech, to that and only that which we desire to call forth in our lives.

So what if you can only do it 10 percent of the time? Would 10 percent more good in your life be better than what you have now? And for all the good you call forth, you are decreasing the negativity you are calling forth. So if things were 90 percent bad and 10 percent good, now they're 80 percent bad and 20 percent good. Keep working it. We can use our word to express gratitude and, by the law of increase by attention and intent, multiply all the good in our lives. Once you have the process started, you only need to continue it.

The attitude of gratitude is nowhere more important than in the area of creating material wealth. The benevolent universe not only doesn't give you more money than you can manage, it also only gives you as much as you can appreciate. Why are so many of us stuck in an attitude of loss, lack, and limitation when the streets are paved with gold?

Because we have not practiced gratitude for everything. The following practice, which I learned from author and wealth-building workshop leader T. Harv Eker, is so powerful that if you are in any way interested in manifesting material wealth, you must begin it now. First, whenever any money comes to you, no matter how big or small, hold it in your hand and shout out loud a powerful verbal expression of your appreciation of the abundance flowing into your life, then do a little dance and hug and kiss yourself.

I do this when I find pennies on the street and you know what? Some days I find several dollars! The effect this has on me when I'm walking around stuck in thoughts of lack and limitation is to remind me that the universe is my resource. Whatever I need can be supplied to me in an instant and from out of nowhere. The training of my consciousness in not only receiving financial good, but in expecting it from unexpected sources, has been a key factor in the great increase in material wealth I have enjoyed. It's so silly, yet so simple. The next time you get a ten-cent check from the phone company or find a penny on the street, or when you open the envelope containing your paycheck, say:

> I make money like bees make honey!
> I love money and money loves me!
> I am a money magnet!
> I live in a world of abundance!
> Money flows through me like fish in the sea!

Before you know it, you will have repatterned your cellular structure out of the consciousness of lack and limitation, and opened it to the awareness that everything you need can be supplied easily and effortlessly.

"DICTUM MEUM PACTUM"—MY WORD IS MY BOND.

"Bond" is defined as a covenant, agreement, pledge, or treaty that fetters or ties things together. Since 1801 it has been the motto of the London Stock Exchange, where all transactions are made without any exchange of written documents. Could someone trust your word the same way?

David Hawkins, M.D., Ph.D., performed a twenty-year study using kinesiology, or muscle testing, to investigate the source of knowledge. It is published in his book *Power vs. Force.* One of his discoveries is that a person's body can be used to test the "yes" or "truth" of any question, regardless of the person's knowledge of the subject matter of the question. The other part of the study showed that words have power. They actually carry a vibration that Hawkins called "1-1000."

Words like "fear," "anger," and "guilt" vibrate in the below-200 range, and he characterizes them as "words of force." Words of force are those words, thoughts, or ideas that create opposition. Words of power, which calibrate above 200 (courage—200; willingness—310; reason—400; love—500), do not create opposition. By not creating a force of opposition, these words have the ability to make a way where there was no way. The reason is that without the equal and opposite force of opposition, all of a person's energy moves forward, toward something.

How often does your word create opposition in a situation or in another person? Or how often does your word deny the truth of your free will? How often do you talk about what you "have to do" and what you've "got to do" instead of what you choose to do and what you get to do?

"I get to go to work today."
"I get to cook dinner today."

"I get to go in early and stay at work late."

"I'm choosing to skip dessert."

"I'm choosing to only speak about my good."

The differences in words we use every day can make a big difference in our lives.

If you "have to" do something today, you'll "have to" do it in the future. Wouldn't you prefer to "get to do" everything you're going to do? Doesn't the sound of that just make everything more inviting? Your words conjure moods, worlds they can inspire or annihilate. Choose to use your words to build your world for the better.

1. Use your "I am" statements to express only the eternal truths of your existence, rather than temporary passing feelings.

    I am outstanding.

    I am perfect, whole, and complete.

    I am divine.

    I am most excellent well!

2. Use your words to name and claim what you desire.

3. Say what you mean.

4. Do what you say.

5. Ask permission to break commitments, and honor a "no."

6. Formally de-commit from commitments you have made to yourself, if you must.

7. Use language of choice rather than force.

    "I get to," rather than "I've got to."

    "I choose to," rather than "I have to."

    "I want to," rather than "I need to."

8. Speak gratefully when you receive any expression of material wealth of any size.

  I make money like bees make honey.

  I love money and money loves me.

  I am a money magnet.

  I live in a world of abundance.

  Wealth flows to me as fish swim in the sea.

9. Choose words that vibrate in the high range of power rather than in the lower vibration of force. Speak like a successful, happy, grateful person. You are one.

TEN

MAKE FEAR YOUR FRIEND

In every challenge, there is a victor. It is either you or your obstacle. And if one condition will stop you, any condition can stop you. When we are weak in the face of a challenge, all our good intentions and even our efforts may come to nothing. So you must learn to be a whatever-it-takes-at-the-time person. You must learn to practice the positive act of allowing no negative story, condition, or obstacle to prevent you from reaching your goal.

If I can show you how to do that, will you do it?

What is fear?

FEAR IS THE ANTICIPATION OF FUTURE PAIN

There is nothing tangible about fear beyond our own sweaty palms, racing heart, and generalized tension. Yet the thing we fear has no existence. You can't touch it or grab hold of it because it lies in an imagined event. Its existence is only in your mind. And it is only in your mind, when your mind is anywhere but where you are.

Right now, bring your attention to this moment. What are you doing? What are you wearing? What do you see? What do you hear? What do you taste? What do you smell? Where is your fear? It is nowhere. In the present moment, we always have everything we require. Eckhart Tolle's book *The Power of Now* delves deeply into our innate tendency to miss our own life because our attention is more often focused on some remembered past or imagined future. It doesn't matter whether the memories or imaginings are positive or negative; what matters is that while we are there, we are missing being here, and here is where our life is.

Do not dwell in the past, do not dream of the future, concentrate the mind on the present moment.

—Buddha

When I was a young actress in my twenties, I was replaced in a show called *The Piano Lesson*, after being on tour for a year, right before the Broadway production. It was devastating, because it was my first nonmusical play and it had been a real coup, written by August Wilson and directed by Lloyd Richardson. Now I was no longer a part of this prestigious and wonderful production. Lloyd had called me to tell me that I was being replaced, and he said it was because they were rewriting my character. But when I saw the play after that, it was written exactly the same way I had played it, and it became clear I was just replaced. I assumed that the problem was in me, not in the particular role.

My fear mounted when a "friend" told me that she heard Lloyd thought I was "difficult." Filled with shame and chagrin, I was afraid to audition for anything for a while. I worked on trying to rebuild my confidence so I could audition again, and I managed to do so, and went on with my life. Until I got a call to audition for Lloyd Richardson again.

It was the role of a lifetime, Maggie in the Tennessee Williams play *Cat on a Hot Tin Roof*. How I had always dreamed of playing that part! But what was the point of even trying? Surely Lloyd would not hire me, since he was predisposed against me. I was torn between my fear of failure and my fantasy of portraying this great character, one of the greatest in the theater.

So what did I do? I acknowledged to myself that Lloyd might very well think of me as having been difficult in the past, but still, he had invited me back. Therefore, I reasoned that my being "difficult" wasn't the most important issue for him—so why should it be for me? He was giving me a chance; I was sure going to take it.

I remembered what the late actor Avon Long had said to me once: "You gotta have 'nuisance value' in this business." What he meant was that you had to be so good at what you did that you were worth the nuisance. I was betting that I was worth the nuisance if they were inviting me to read. I went into that room scared, but ready to express my talent, which was what the audience would ultimately experience.

Feedback from that audition was outstanding. Had that production come to fruition, I have no doubt that I would have been cast as Maggie the Cat.

Do it in Fear.

Gavin de Becker calls fear our gift. Who would you be without it? Your fear calls your attention to features you need to watch in any unknown frontier. Without fear, how could you monitor the fact that you are growing and expanding into your greater self?

Think about it. Do you fear driving on the freeway in your car? Do you fear eating in restaurants? Do you fear your coworkers? Probably not, because those situations are familiar to you. Put your car on the German speedway, the Autobahn, though, or eat strange-looking food from a street vendor in a foreign country, and more likely than not, some degree of fear appears. Fear lets you know that you are growing. Fear lets you know that you have reached the edge of your envelope of experience. And isn't that where you want to live all the time? Don't you want to be constantly meeting, living up to, and conquering new experiences, new worlds? Don't you want to create a new self?

Then fear is your best friend. Fear is the signal that you are on the right track. Face it: If you're not doing something unknown, you're just re-arranging all the old books in your library of limited awareness. Do you want that library to expand? Do you want to write some new stories?

Then let fear be your constant and faithful companion. In fact, invite fear into your life where you used to run from it or push it away. Fight-or-flight need no longer be your only response to the unknown. You can turn fight-or-flight into

FLOW.

Flow: a new "F" word for the fear stimulus. You no longer need to stand up to your fear and conquer it, nor must you run from your fear hoping that courage will one day come. You can, instead, choose differently and Flow with your fear, and

Do it in fear.

You want to be a whatever-it-takes-at-the-time person?

Do it in fear.

You want to claim the life you deserve?

Do it in fear.

Rebecca had been a very successful actress. One season, one of the most prestigious theaters in the United States invited her to star in an entire season of the great classic roles. "It was the most exciting event of my life. The rest of the cast were extraordinarily talented people whom I admired, and the artistic director was a handsome genius I fell madly in love with." Becka and the artistic director began an affair, and love and work thrived until he fell for the ingenue in the upcoming production and not only dumped Becka but scrapped the season for plays more suitable to his new leading lady. The blow was so severe that Becka stopped working in the theater. She had become a masseuse and an acting student when I met her.

Her fear had overwhelmed her. She not only couldn't trust the process of casting and acting, but she couldn't trust herself to not fall apart if it didn't work out the way she planned. She excelled in acting class, where she felt safe, but she would not even venture to an audition because, she said, "Those contracts aren't worth the paper they're printed on."

Becka had taken one understandably horrible and humiliating experience and projected it across all her future days. My task was not to prove her wrong, but to prove to her that, even if she was right, it didn't justify abandoning her dream.

"Do it in fear," I told her. "If you audition, you really don't know what will happen; but if you don't audition, you absolutely know what will happen." I asked if she valued certainty over possibility. I'm asking you the same thing.

For instance, would you rather have an absolute "no" or a qualified "maybe"?

For most of my life, I felt safer with the no. So much so that, like Rebecca, I would turn myself down rather than risk giving someone else the chance to turn me down. Of course I also prevented them having the chance to give me a yes, too.

What's the risk?

Yes, it hurts to be told no—unless you can reframe it, as James did. James was a telemarketer, the best cold-call salesman I ever met. I asked what his secret was. He explained, "You start one day with this batch of cards with names and numbers. Ninety-nine percent of them are duds. After a day of working, thinking that way, you wanna kill yourself. But it hit me that if only one in a hundred calls was a sale, I better make as many calls as possible so I could get more winners. Now, instead of thinking, 'Oh, I've got ninety-eight more hang-ups to go,' I switched to, 'One down, only ninety-eight to go and then I get my sale!' Now I actually average more than that because now, instead of dreading each failure, I'm looking forward to getting them behind me so I can get to the success. And my percentage of successes has jumped up to ten in every hundred."

What a great idea: seeing each failure as a step closer to success.

Are you ready to do that?

In Chapter 3, I used the acronym, "Face Everything And Recover" as a method for meeting fear. Here, we will use as a definition of fear

False
Evidence
Appearing
Real.

Rebecca thought one painful affair and a bad ending to one job was evidence of a real failure in her career. But James knew that ninety-nine calls that didn't net him any profit were just evidence of the inevitability of success.

> A man who fears suffering is already suffering from what he fears.
> —Michel de Montaigne

Yet we do fear suffering, and pain, and loss; and we cannot escape any of them by either fight or flight. My favorite opening of a book is the beginning of M. Scott Peck's *The Road Less Traveled*. Peck says life is difficult. When you accept that, everything else is easy. Why do we elevate, adore, admire, and highly compensate athletes and entertainers? Because they do what we believe we could never do. They model the path of being the hero in their own lives.

Are you ready to be the hero of your own life?

Write down ten things you most fear doing.

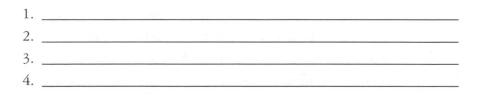

1. _____
2. _____
3. _____
4. _____

5. _____
6. _____
7. _____
8. _____
9. _____
10. _____

Now pick one and write down a description of the absolute worst thing that could happen to you if you did that thing.

_____
_____
_____
_____
_____
_____

Now: Is your heart racing, are your palms sweaty, are you trembling in terror that it could ever happen?

Then the worst is over.

The mind does not know the difference between a "real" or "remembered/imagined" event. Because of the psychosomatic connection, you have just lived the emotional reality of one of your worst nightmares. How are you doing? You're still here. You survived it. Congratulate yourself!

Now let's do it again. Only this time, describe it turning out the absolute best way possible.

_____
_____
_____
_____
_____

Now how do you feel: excited, invigorated, like you could actually do the thing you fear?

Doing it in fear is a powerful way to transform your cellular pattern and create new pathways that can allow you to change the habitual autonomic responses formed by early fearful experiences.

As I have been writing this book, each chapter I have worked on has shown up in my current life. Of course, since I lived the chapters as I wrote them, the two most difficult chapters were Dying Daily and Fear.

The two years I spent performing in *Caroline, or Change* gave me an intimate connection to fear and dying. I could not have participated in that show had I not continually and consistently acted in spite of my fear, and then, having done so, continued to surrender to the daily death of the old self that was being replaced by my new behaviors and circumstances. At every step of the way, something in the process of *Caroline* evoked fear and then required the death of the old self to surmount.

First there was the negative press, which preceded my arrival in New York. I chose to come to town in spite of it. Then one day the director went from calling it an "ensemble show" to telling me that I was the event of the show, and I had to die to my identity as an ensemble member and become what I had never experienced: the headlining star of a Broadway show. This was foreign territory for me. I was also learning new ways to sing, and working more hours than seemed humanly possible, all of which required the death of the old identity of myself to be replaced by someone who was as yet unknown to me.

One thing I experienced during these daily deaths was a loss of physical control, in which my voice sometimes did strange and unnatural things in the most bizarre moments onstage. After consulting with many physicians and discovering that there was no physical problem, I could only attribute this phenomenon to me, still trying to do things in my old way while a new me was birthing. Now I had to choose what to do, and chart my own course. Nobody had any answers for me. I could stay home and rest, of course, which I did for about a week, but it had no real effect on the random loss of my voice control. My fear was great: Here I was with my name above the title of a Broadway show and my voice just went wonky. Could I have dropped out of the show? I don't know. Did I ever even consider it? No.

If I had been asked to leave, would I have left? Absolutely. But that was not the case. The choice was mine to make, and I chose to stay and learn to flow with the scary new feeling, the loss of control. I relied on an old mantra of mine: "I can outact any singer any day." Did some audience members find it distracting? I'm sure they did. Did it prevent people from having the powerful and transformational experience of the show? No. There was never a performance at which someone did not stand and stand at the stage door just so they could share with me their deep and profound gratitude for my expression of Caroline. Does that diminish the feelings of those people who wanted to hear me sound better? No.

But what it showed me was that, despite my fear and even at my worst, I could still be in the service of the divine. It gave me an opportunity to die to my ego's perception of itself at its best, and come to know that, at my worst, it could still be experienced as somebody's best.

How many things have you chosen not to do because of your fear that it would not be good enough? It won't be the best; it won't be perfect; someone will say it wasn't good enough. I know from my own experience that being useful and of service and inspiring and powerful does not automatically bring out the ego's sense of "the best." Being of true service means showing up, no matter what. When you show up no matter what, and even in your worst mood, spirit, voice, health, whatever, you allow something else to come through. When you show up maimed and frightened and insecure, you strengthen the muscle of faith and courage. It cannot build its strength if you're always doing what you know how to do. Even physical muscles must be challenged beyond their comfortable ability so that they can grow to greater strength and size. Athletes work their muscles right up to the point of failure.

How often have you consciously worked up to failure so that your own mental, psychological, and spiritual muscles can grow in size and strength?

It is anathema for individuals to do such a thing: to falter, to fail, to fall, to show their dirty laundry, to allow others to see them wipe out miserably. But without that, there is no growth.

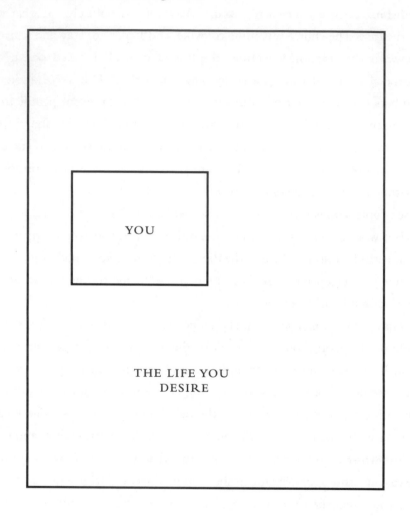

You live in a box right now, but the box you want to live in is a lot bigger. You can't get there, however, without tearing down the walls of the little box.

Do it in fear.

Know that your worst is always somebody else's best. Know that just because you can model the perfect jump shot, that you might still not be a model for great pass interception, or rebounding. Know that life is always expecting something more of you. When you show up no matter what, you allow life to do, through you, what could not be done without you.

It is by our fears and obstacles that the best part of us is allowed to shine through. It is interesting to me that it was also René Descartes who first demonstrated how a rainbow is formed. To have a rainbow, you must have simultaneous sunshine and rain, but without clouds there could be no rainbows. The thicker and denser the cloud, the greater the refraction and reflection of the colors of the rainbow's spectrum. In fact, because the rainbow is a specific distribution of colors produced, based upon the reference point or eye of the observer, no two people can see the same rainbow, except in a photograph, which records what was seen by the eye of a single observer with a camera.

What for you is a death-defying act may show the world the full scope and spectrum of the rainbow of your gifts and talents. But without the cloud, there can be no refraction.

Our ego, in its attempt to maintain control of things, holds the world as a static thing and then relates to its projection. But the world is constantly changing, and if you respond from your fear, many times things will go wrong simply because, from the space of fear, you are no longer seeing the situation, and when you do respond, it is to a situation or circumstance that no longer exists in the way you have recalled it. Your fear has created false evidence, to which you now respond as if it were real.

What false evidence is appearing real to you now? That if you do the thing you fear, you will never recover from the humiliation? The more important question to ask is: Who will you be after you recover from the humiliation? Is there any great hero who hasn't recovered from a great humiliation? Isn't that the first qualification for being a hero?

"Hero" is a Greek word originally meaning "demigod." The hero in mythology was one who protected or served, usually at great risk to the self. Hero status was not bestowed until after death. My own personal sheroes/heroes are people who have died to their egoic idea of self and thus created movements that have thereby transformed the consciousness of the world. Each of them faced a fear of showing something "unattractive" in themselves, and by doing so, made it okay for others to do the same, the ultimate effect of which has served and protected many people by destigmatizing a condition or situation.

Eve Ensler went public about her own childhood sexual molestation, writing a play entitled *The Vagina Monologues.* This theatrical production became the World V-Day Initiative, which has raised millions of dollars to protect women and to stop violence against them. The play opens with some humor about the dreaded "V" word. Ensler faced her fear and said it anyway.

Author, educator, and activist Larry Kramer came forward and admitted to being HIV positive at a time when worldwide fear of the AIDS virus had ostracized millions. He's still here, twenty-five years later, and along the way he has inspired the creation of ACT UP, Gay Men's Health Crisis, and dozens of organizations that serve and protect the men, women, and children affected by this plague. He faced his fear and did it anyway.

Even the worst possible thing is a thing of your creation. You have called it forth so that you can experience a greater sense of your own being. Embrace it. Let fear be your constant companion and bedfellow. Let fear remind you that you are always seeking your highest and greatest good, constantly laying claim on the life you deserve.

Here is my new translation of the Twenty-third Psalm.

Though every day as I walk around
my ears are filled with words and thoughts of
lack and limitation,
those words will fall on deaf ears.
Because I know that I am divinely guided,
directed and protected in every moment of my life.
My blessings are pouring down on me like the sun
and the rain from the skies.
I can give copiously from my overflow.
I am ready to receive my good.

And here's a knock, knock joke for you:

Knock, knock.

Who's there?

Goodness and mercy.

Knock, knock.

Who's there?

Goodness and mercy, following you all the days of your life, because truly, all things are working together for your highest and greatest good.

1. F = A of FP

   Fear is the anticipation of future pain.

2. *Flow*

3. Diagram of the boxes

4. Do it in fear.

5. Write down the worst and best thing that could happen if you do what you're afraid to do. Then do it anyway.

6. Do one thing you fear every day.

| ELEVEN |

MAKE SUCCESS INEVITABLE

Are you ready to drop the drama and claim the life you deserve?

Yes, or Yes?

Are you ready to stand in the knowledge of the inevitability of your success, despite all appearances to the contrary?

Yes, or Yes?

If you said Yes, I stand in agreement with you that it's already done.

And if you're still not sure, I stand in agreement that you are well on your way.

Evolution is defined by *The Cambridge Dictionary* as "the way in which living things change and develop over millions of years," or "a gradual process of change and development." It comes from the Latin word for "unroll" or "unfold." Evolution does not, in fact cannot, leave any of us behind. Whether you choose to unfold gradually or in an instant, the choice is always yours. The following practices show you what you have to look forward to. We are all predestined to our highest and greatest good, but we can, of course, choose to resist that and stick to the drama. What do you choose?

Before you decide, let's get a glimpse of what's in store. Take two pieces of paper and draw on each a circle that fills the entire page.

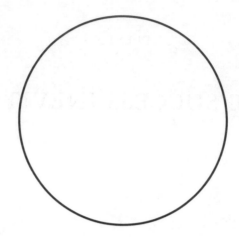

In the middle of each circle, now, make a smaller circle the size of a quarter.

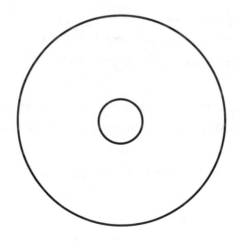

Now write your name in the very center. We are going to create your circles of connection and extension.

On the top of the page of the first circle, write: "My circle of advisers." On the top of the page of the second circle, write, "The extensions of me."

Now, in the first circle, write the names of all those persons, living or dead, whom you would choose to be your advisers as you move toward your greater yet to be. How about Leonardo da Vinci, Einstein, Noam Chomsky, Oprah Winfrey? From whom would you seek counsel?

The phrase "six degrees of separation" refers to the theory that each of us is only six contacts away from any other person in the world. Literally, if you connected to someone and they connected to someone else and we carried this forward six times, you could reach anyone in the world. There is a powerful game called the Beehive that uses this principle, allowing every player of the game to get something they want by using the resources and connections of every other player. As you write down the names of the people you want to connect to, you send out a message that creates the bridge to connect you. Don't be shy. This is your dream, and you get to play God here. Heck, put Her on your council!

Now look at your circle. How would you feel if those people were advising you every day? Do you think you'd be able to get the job done? Is there anything you wouldn't be able to accomplish?

So what's stopping you? They are already your council. You chose their names because you are already connected. For every name you listed, there are millions you left out. Why? Because all these connections, past, present, and future, are waiting to unfold from inside you. Some part of you may be saying, "But that's not possible."

If you limit your choices only to what seems possible or
reasonable, you disconnect yourself from what you truly want,
and all that is left is a compromise.

—Robert Fritz

Create your council. Then move on to the second circle and begin to write all of the extensions, or brands, of you. This is a powerful exercise given to me by Steve Krash, head of marketing for the *New York Times*. Steve said, "In today's world you have to think of yourself as a brand, and what are all the franchises that extend from you? Your knowledge, your experiences; somebody somewhere needs it, and may be willing to pay you for it."

Face it: We all like a little drama. It makes us feel alive. It's what we're looking for in movies and soap operas. Instead of suffering through it, then, turn it into a profit. There have been some marvelous cases of people turning what some might consider a handicap into a lucrative entrepreneurial business. Mark Victor Hansen became a best-selling writer without writing a book: He simply collected the stories of other great people he'd met and created the "Chicken Soup" series, possibly the biggest publishing franchise ever. Somebody turned their own admitted ignorance and dumb luck into a plethora of bestselling "Dummy" manuals.

Council of Light

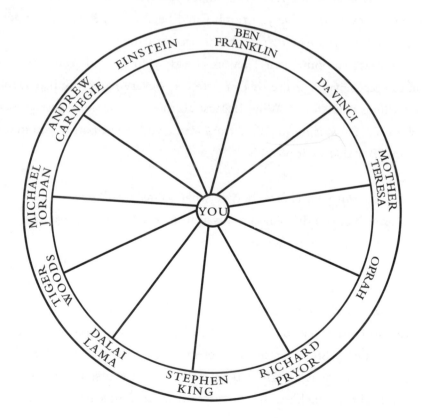

You've done something better or worse or differently than anybody else, and there is probably a business in it. Write it down. At the edge of the circle, write all the extensions of you. Is there a cookbook, a photojournalism book, a radio show, a cable show, an Internet sales site, a consulting business, a design, a business, a travel guide, some language teaching method, an intricate dance step, a nighttime melody, a love song, a poem, an invention, a product? If it works for you, it'll probably work for somebody else. You are sitting on a gold mine. It's you.

And if you finish your list and you think, "Yeah, but I don't know how to turn this into that stuff," you know what?

You are on the right track!!!!!

Extensions of Self

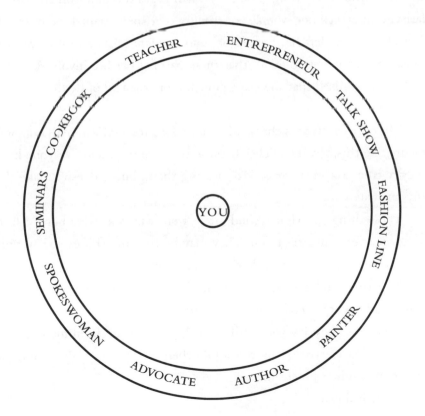

Because if you are finally thinking about creating things that you don't know how to create, you have finally stepped out of the world you have been living in, and from the edge of this cliff, "the ground will rise to meet you or you will learn how to fly."

Do you feel more alive when you think about these new possibilities, however impossible or unfamiliar they seem? The test is the aliveness. If it wakes you up and inspires you, even if you don't have the first clue what to do, this is what you were meant to do.

Now you have designed your wheel. That's your wheel, and you're in the driver's seat now.

What would your life be like if you got up every day and did something from your wheel? Would that be a world worth waking up to, no matter what other circumstances were going on around you?

To quote Mary Manin Morrissey, "If you know how to do it, it's not worthy of you. It's not big enough." When I said this at a women's summit last year, it struck one woman so strongly that she e-mailed me to say that a week later she left her home, job, and husband of twenty-five years because she knew how to do all that these parts of her life involved, and she had finally realized that she was so much more than all of that.

You are too.

The only constant is change. If you're not growing, you're dying. Statements like this become clichés because they are true, and everyone knows they're true. You may get sick of hearing them, but it doesn't make them any less true.

These things on your second circle were why you were born. They're what you were put here to do. They may be the only things you were put here to do. And if you don't do them, they don't get done.

Now that you know what you want, let's add some leverage to boost the power and possibility of completing your plan.

Who else, besides you, will be helped by your fulfillment of your dream? What are you going to do for others as a result of living out your truest and highest potential?

Write it down:

_____

_____

_____

_____

_____

And now that you know whom it will help, let's up the stakes. What will happen if you don't fulfill your dream? Why is it imperative that you succeed?

The sometimes-sad fact is that most of us are willing to do more for others than we are willing to do for ourselves. Instead of bemoaning that, use it. Make it work for you. Say: "I will do this because if I do, it will help so-and-so to . . ." Whom will your success help?

Write it down.

_____

_____

_____

_____

_____

We have to stay on track. Every opportunity that comes along is just another distraction unless it moves you closer to doing what was put into your heart to do. The thoughts you have had while reading this manual, the exercises you have done, have sent out powerful vibrations to the universe to create exactly what you want, and with "no substitutions." So don't get distracted if somebody next to you gets promoted. Think about it: Had you gotten that promotion, would it have been a move toward, or away from, the life you've now decided to create? If it's not moving you toward what you want, bow in gratitude to the sign that what you desire is on the way.

Speak the affirmation:

Man's rejection is the universe's protection.

And know that it is true.

Now that you have called up your own unique, divine life, everything that doesn't fit into it will fall away.

I once heard a sermon from a minister in Texas who had a metaphor for every circumstance in your life. He said that the dark empty space between the life you used to live and the life that you're about to live is akin to the space between the scenes of a stage play, when the stagehands come in and move things around. You might not know that a man or woman from the last scene is being replaced with a new one in the next scene. And for the play to go on seamlessly, the stagehands need the cover of darkness to re-arrange the scenery.

Your new life won't look like this one. Get ready to let it go. Are you ready to let go of the old to make room for the new?

Are you ready to do things poorly until you can do them well?

Because anything worth doing is worth doing poorly until you can do it well.

There will be failure. And as you rise higher, the failures may be bigger. But as you manage each larger failure, you will acquire the tools for greater success. You only need one yes; so what if you get fifty thousand nos before you get it?

You can tell yourself that each "no" is moving you closer to the one "yes." And it will be true.

DON'T TURN YOURSELF DOWN

The world may be ready and willing to do it, so you must never do it. You must be your own best advocate. Imagine that. You want to know how to never need anyone else's approval ever again?

Approve of yourself.

I'm not talking about an attitude. I'm talking about a practice of con-sciously, daily congratulating yourself and counting up all of the great things you do. We all desire approval, and if we depend on it from any out-side source, we give our power away. Most of us don't have that much to give away. I bet you know what it feels like to finish a project or cook a meal and wait for somebody to pat you on the back and say, "Good job." If they do, that's great, but most of the time, people are too caught up in their own dramas to even take notice of your efforts. So you are left on the roller coaster of emotion, going up and down depending upon someone else's ability to turn their attention, for a moment, from themselves to you. And really, all of us are focused on ourselves. When we do focus outside ourselves, it's generally to get something for ourselves. That's not a bad thing. It's what we're here to do. Each of us is here to so thoroughly purify our inner thoughts and feelings that our world becomes a reflection of the peace and harmony that radiates from within. How often does your world look peaceful and harmonious? When it does, it is a reflection of you.

If someone is complimenting you, it reflects their appreciation of themselves. So why can't you do this for yourself? When you bypass the coffee or the candy, give yourself a hand, literally. Put your hands together and clap for yourself. When you finish a project and you know you've done your best, pat your own back. Tell yourself: "Congratulations, I am proud of myself!" Write it down. Keep a journal of your daily successes. It will help you in remembering what to stay grateful for. Right now, today, what can you congratulate yourself for? Pick ten things. Write them down.

1. _____
2. _____
3. _____
4. _____
5. _____
6. _____
7. _____
8. _____
9. _____
10. _____

Psychologists have found that couples in healthy relationships have one hundred or more positive exchanges every day: each one a touch, a look, a gesture, a word. Couples in unhealthy relationships, however, have one hundred or more negative exchanges a day: a cross word, a scowl, some mocking gesture, a demeaning look.

I believe the most important relationship we have is with ourselves, and until we can practice being loving and approving of ourselves, we will attract only partners who reflect the way we feel about and treat ourselves. Would you choose yourself as a partner? Why not? Everything you want your partner to be to you, you must be to yourself. Are you ready to do that?

How we treat ourselves is the truest reflection of who we really are. Approve of yourself every day, and write it down. Make your own success journal to list all the accomplishments you fulfill each and every day.

Throughout this book I have urged you to write things down. Why? Because I believe that words are thoughts made physical. Making your thoughts physical is a way of making your inner intentions real, giving birth to your emotional life. And when you write, your hand and your mind work together, making you more careful, more true to your spiritual self. And because writing is action, the act of writing is an act that requires attention; writing down your thought focuses your attention and helps to make it happen.

Write down your self-approval and, whether you believe all you say or not, in time it will become the truth of who you are.

Each day, acknowledge the power of nature working in and through your life. The basic four directional prayer practiced by the congregants of the Morningstar Community is a powerful morning practice to keep us remembering how we should live in each moment of each day. If you will practice these steps before ever opening your mouth in any situation, your world will be transformed.

TO THE EAST: I show up.
TO THE SOUTH: I listen.
TO THE WEST: I speak my truth.
TO THE NORTH: I release all attachment to outcome.

What does it mean to show up? It means that we come to every moment as empty fertile soil waiting to be impregnated by the divine. What does it mean to listen? It is to be receptive to all that is around us and all that is being offered to us. What does it mean to speak my truth? It means to give only what is real and true and to give no attention to the transitory appearance of things. What does it mean to release all attachment to outcome? It means to do all this without expectation of reward but in confidence that only your good can come to you.

So: Ready, _____, _____.

I know how you filled it in. But rethink it as:

Ready, fire, aim.

To succeed, jump as quickly at opportunities as you do at conclusions.

—Benjamin Franklin

Most people wait for the exact perfect situation, circumstance, or moment before they do anything. Well, that moment comes around once in a millennium, and if you miss it, boo-hoo.

Stop waiting! If you shoot toward your dreams, you can straighten out your aim along the way. If you still don't know what you really want to do, fire at something new and let the aim find you.

There is an implicate order seeking to unfold as your life. All you have to do is to let it unfold and remove whatever is in its way.

Here's an exercise I do every year on my birthday. I no longer remember who first shared it with me, but I've been doing it for many years. In the spirit and vibration of a new year of life, I sit down in meditation and write all that I plan to give myself in the coming year. I write a detailed list of all that will be accomplished by my next birthday. A year later I open the envelope and am overwhelmed at the gifts I have given myself.

Believe in yourself; invest in yourself. If you want to have a new relationship, new house, car, business, whatever, find it, create it, and let the way to do it reveal itself to you. If you want to go to a certain school or work for a certain company, go there and meet the people, be a part of it, and let the way that it will come to pass reveal itself to you.

Show up where you want to be, as who you want to be, every day.

Reverend Karen Weingard presides over the Lighthouse Church in Golem, California, just outside San Diego. She is one of the most beautiful and radiant beings I have ever had the fortune to behold. Almost seventy years old, she doesn't look a day over forty. She believes that every day is a cause for celebration. She has taken it upon herself to represent the ministry of beauty every moment of her life.

Every day she fills her hair with jewels, adorns her face with jewels, and dons colorful, bejeweled suits and gowns that reflect the beauty that flows deeply from inside her soul. No matter what is going on in the world, Karen looks like she is always on her way to the finest fairy-tale ball.

We live in a world where newspapers and TVs constantly blare the bad news, the disasters, the statistics, telling us over and over why we can't have it our way without doing it somebody else's way. You must consciously and proactively counteract their effects by filling your mind with the thoughts that remind you of why you *can* have it exactly your way.

If you've ever been to the Carnegie House on East 91st Street and Fifth Avenue in New York City, you will see that Andrew Carnegie had his affirmations engraved into the wood and marble that decorated his home. If it's good enough for Andrew Carnegie, is it good enough for you? Put your affirmations in front of your bed, on the bathroom mirror, on the front door, anyplace your eye lands often. Let it land on a thought that can uplift you and remind you that all things are working for your good.

Nothing stopped you from reading all the way through this book; nothing can stop you from using this reading experience to your best advantage. Success is not a nonrenewable resource, like oil. If you are very successful, that doesn't mean someone else must be less so. Furthermore, nobody can hoard success or prevent you from getting yours. Nobody holds the rights to it; nobody has a patent on it; nobody controls the amount of it;

it is the quintessential free-market commodity and it's yours for the taking. Therefore, if something is holding you back, you need only to change that condition.

What could that condition be? Fear of failure? Get over it. Low self-esteem? Get over it.

I did.

My own experience of lacking self-esteem makes me an expert. It propelled me to success—that's right!—if only because my need to prove myself "good enough" kept me working harder, faster, better than anyone else. My own fear led me to acquire the skills and tools that allowed me to successfully manage being a single mother of four while simultaneously acting on Broadway, teaching, lecturing, giving concerts, performing in clubs, recording albums, and writing this book.

Actually, I believe that strong egos have stopped more people from reaching their potential than neuroses have. What is the ego? The ego is a great sentry. Its whole purpose is to defend its borders and maintain the status quo. Consequently it is always yelling "Watch out!" or "No, that's dangerous!" or "Don't go there!" or "Keep them away!" It keeps us from walking out into traffic, but it also keeps us from stepping out of the boundaries of our known universe and into the unknown where all genius lies.

How many talented people do you know with dozens of logical, rational reasons and explanations for why they cannot achieve their desired goals?

Are you one of them?

One of the problems is the cultural mandate to always be/do our best. The truth is, we can never do less than "our best" at any one time. And that "best" varies from day to day, moment to moment. Your best when you have a headache or a cold or were up all night will be different from your best when you made love first thing in the morning or went to the gym for a dynamite workout.

We knock ourselves off track when we judge one "best" as better than another "best." Ideally, when we become experts in our chosen field, we must reach the point where we know that our worst is better than many people's best; we have studied and practiced to make that so. Then we let go and *do* what we do best—as best we can. And all the study and practice comes into play: Our experience enables us to do things well.

Does illness just wipe out years of study and practice? No. The true fact is that the best can be done even when we're not at our best.

One of my acting instructors, William Esper, often said actors do their best work when they're exhausted, because then the ego shuts down and can't get in their way.

Let nothing get in your way.

When I taught drawing and painting, I used methods from Dr. Betty Edwards's book *Drawing on the Right Side of the Brain*: exercises like copying paintings upside-down or drawing without looking at the paper, various techniques to shut off the ego so the artist's real brilliance can emerge.

Early in this book, I said that 80 percent of success is simply showing up. Statistically, many people rise to the top of their companies because their lack of ego quelled any desire to leave their employment, so as time passed, their experience and tenure buoyed them to the top.

Am I saying your ego is bad for you? No. I'm saying that when you're willing to show up, even when you're not what you consider at your "best," very often the best can still be accomplished.

Martha was a skillful and caring psychotherapist in a successful practice for twenty years. At age fifty-five, though, she began to question the methods she had been using after one of her patients committed suicide. The incident flung her into a depression, which I call a dark night of the soul, that threatened her entire practice. For weeks she canceled all her appointments, feeling unqualified to help others, since she couldn't even help herself. You see, Martha's model of "good psychotherapist" was a person who demonstrated "good mental health." She had certainly had her own trials and tribulations before, but she had always carried on, never losing her balance. Now that her confidence was shaken, her ego was telling her that she was no use to herself or her clients.

I asked her what would happen if she just showed up for her patients' scheduled therapy sessions anyway. Her ego scared her too much to con-template that: She was sure she would compromise her patients' welfare be-cause they had come to depend upon her rock-hard foundation of clarity and certainty to help them through their emotional troubles. Couldn't some good come from giving them an opportunity to experience her in an-other way? I asked. Martha considered this. She had to admit it was possi-ble, but felt that the risk of damage far outweighed any benefits the clients might derive. I asked, "What about the benefits you might derive?"

Martha didn't understand how that could help. "You're birthing a new life, shedding an old skin," I said, "and sometimes in life, we have to do that in an awkward place, and recover on the road, and keep moving." I asked her to risk showing up for her clients because of the good it might do for her: She would know exactly what she was capable of accomplishing, even in her darkest hour. Who knows how that could help others? Yet, who knows that it would not?

This was not a one-time conversation. Her ego had the upper hand: the horror stories; her medical, legal, and moral responsibilities; her habit of of-fering only her "best." One night as she lay in bed weeping, the phone rang. It was one of her patients who had worked very hard to get her home num-ber. Martha tried to get off the phone and go back to wallowing in self-pity, but the patient wouldn't let her go.

"I was pissed, I was angry, how dare this person violate my privacy! But as I stopped thinking about me, and listened, I realized that the patient was getting a great benefit just being on the line with me. It didn't even matter that I was still drowning in my own misery." Martha learned that at her worst, she still had something to give that was of great value to another hu-man being. Right then, she made the commitment to show up for all her other appointments, regardless of her personal state of mind, and to do her best. And that's what she did.

Martha began to show up for her clients while she was still uncertain how to deal with her own emotional problems, and somehow the divine flowed through her and the best was done, even while she wasn't at "her best."

Are you willing to just show up, no matter what?
Why not? Write it:

_____

_____

_____

_____

I guarantee you, your ego is talking you out of it. You see, when you commit to showing up no matter what, ego can't take the credit. If you become a success on your "bad" day, how can ego justify that? You've just put it out of a job. Because ego knows the right way to get a thing done, and getting things done the "wrong" way does not compute. You're not authorized to even try that.

Ego keeps you operating in a limited number of ways to create success, when there are really an infinite number of ways to have exactly what you want. Ego locks you in the drama of specific parameters for how things must be.

When you rise above your ego and

Get Over Yourself!

you allow life to bring you everything you require. You move from living your drama to living your dharma. Eastern philosophers say that to live the dharma is to be in the flow, where the entire universe supports what you do.

When we trade drama for dharma, we cease making the disconnected efforts; we get off the treadmill of earning and deserving and striving and never arriving. Then, what is ours can come to and through us with grace and ease. We must be willing to stop asking what and how much we can expect from life; instead we must be what life expects us to be.

Many wise people have graciously let us see what life expects us to be. A Cherokee blessing says:

> *May you live long enough*
> *to know why you were born.*

And I add:

> *And may you be willing*
> *to get over yourself,*
> *to fulfill it.*

Namaste.
From the divine place within me,
I salute and honor the divine within you.
—Tonya Pinkins

1. Circles of Believing

    A. Your council

    B. Extensions of you

2. Man's rejection is _____.

3. D. T. Y. D.

    Don't Turn Yourself Down

4. Four-directional prayer

5. *Ready, fire, aim*

6. God's stagehands

7. Knock, knock!

| BIBLIOGRAPHY |

Beckwith, Michael. 2000. *40 Day Mind Fast Soul Feast*. Texas: Devorss & Company.

The Holy Bible

Britten, Rhonda. 2004. *Change Your Life in 30 Days*. New York: Perigee.

Britten, Rhonda. 2002. *Fearless Living*. New York: Perigee.

Britten, Rhonda. 2004. *Fearless Loving*. New York: Dutton.

Cameron, Julia. 2002. *The Artist's Way: A Spiritual Path to Higher Creativity (Inner Workbook)*. New York: Tarcher/Putnam.

Clark, Glenn. 1989. *The Man Who Tapped the Secrets of the Universe*. Virginia: University of Science and Philosophy.

Edwards, Betty. 1999. *Drawing on the Right Side of the Brain: A Course in Enhancing Creativity and Artistic Confidence*. New York: Tarcher/Putnam.

Emoto, Masaru. 2004. *The Hidden Messages in Water*. Hillsboro, Ore.: Beyond Words Publishing.

Frankl, Viktor E. 1985. *Man's Search for Meaning*. New York: Washington Square Press.

Fritz, Robert. 1991. *Creating: A Practical Guide to the Creative Process and How to Use It to Create Anything.* New York: Ballantine.

Hansen, Mark Victor, and Robert G. Allen. 2002. *The One Minute Millionaire.* New York: Harmony.

Hawkins, David R. 2002. *Power vs. Force: The Hidden Determinants of Human Behavior.* London: Hay House.

The books of Ernest Holmes, including *Science of Mind; Creative Mind: Tapping the Power Within* (Square One Classics); *How to Change Your Life* (with Michael Beckwith); *How to Use the Science of Mind; Living the Science of Mind; This Thing Called You; Mind; Creative Mind and Success* (The New Thought Library Series); *Thoughts Are Things: The Things in Your Life and the Thoughts that Are Behind* (with Willis Kinnear).

Jaworski, Joseph, and Betty S. Flowers. 1998. *Synchronicity: The Inner Path of Leadership.* San Francisco: Berrett-Koehler.

Johnson, Spencer. 1992. *"Yes" or "No": The Guide to Better Decisions.* New York: HarperCollins.

Liberman, Jacob. *Light: Medicine of the Future.*

Liberman, Jacob. *Take Off Your Glasses and See.*

Liberman, Jacob. 2001. *Wisdom from an Empty Mind.* With Erik Liberman. Sedona, Ariz.: Empty Mind Publications.

The books of Neville, including *The Power of Awareness; Awakened Imagination/The Search; Your Faith Is Your Fortune; Seedtime and Harvest; Law and the Promise; Resurrection; Immortal Man: A Compilation of Lectures.*

Pert, Candace B. 1997. *Molecules of Emotion: The Science Behind Mind-Body Medicine.* New York: Touchstone.

Talbot, Michael. 1991. *The Holographic Universe.* New York: HarperCollins.

Tolle, Eckhart. 1999. *The Power of Now: A Guide to Spiritual Enlightenment.* Novarto, Cal.: New World Library.

Walsch, Neale Donald. 1995. "The Little Soul and the Sun," in *Conversations with God: An Uncommon Dialogue,* Book I. New York: Putnam.

Williamson, Marianne. 1996. *A Return to Love: Reflections on the Principles of "A Course in Miracles."* New York: Perennial.

Rhonda Britten: *www.fearlessliving.org*
T Harv Eker: *www.peakpotentials.com*
Mitchell May: *www.mitchellmay.com*
Michael Beckwith: *www.agapelive.com*
Ishmael Tetteh, the Etherean mission in Ghana:
   www.oneminutemillionaire.com
Mary Manin Morrissey
Sandra Morningstar: *www.morningstarcommunity.org*
Byron Katie: *www.thework.com*
Guru Satchitananda: *www.santmat.org*
Omega Institute: *www.eomega.org*

When I despair, I remember that all through history the way of truth and love has always won. There have been tyrants and murderers and for a time they seem invincible but in the end, they always fall—think of it, ALWAYS.

—Mahatma Gandhi